The Women Troubadours

The Women Troubadours

MEG BOGIN

PADDINGTON PRESS LTD

THE TWO CONTINENTS
PUBLISHING GROUP

A totas las valens femnas
qu'an cantat ses estre cantadas.

To all the valiant women
who have sung and gone unsung.

Library of Congress Cataloging in Publication Data

Bogin, Meg.
    The women troubadours.

    Bibliography: p.
    Includes index.
    1. Provençal poetry – Women authors – History and criticism.
    2. Troubadours. I. Title.
    PC3308.B64   849'.1'04   75-22960

ISBN 0 8467 0113 8
Copyright © 1976 Paddington Press Ltd
Filmset by Filmtype Services Limited
Scarborough, England
Printed in the U.S.A.
Designed by Richard Johnson

IN THE UNITED STATES
PADDINGTON PRESS LTD
TWO CONTINENTS PUBLISHING GROUP
30 East 42 Street
New York City, N.Y. 10017

IN THE UNITED KINGDOM
PADDINGTON PRESS LTD
231 The Vale
London W3 7QS

IN CANADA
distributed by
RANDOM HOUSE OF CANADA LTD
5390 Ambler Drive, Mississauga
Ontario L4 W 1Y7

TABLE OF CONTENTS

ACKNOWLEDGMENTS   6
INTRODUCTION   8
THE ESSAY
   Historical Background   20
   Courtly Love: A New Interpretation   37
   The Women Troubadours   63

THE POEMS
   A Word on the Translations   77
   Pronunciation Guide   78
   Tibors   80
   Countess of Dia   82
   Almucs de Castelnau and Iseut de Capio   92
   Azalais de Porcairages   94
   Maria de Ventadorn   98
   Alamanda   102
   Garsenda   108
   Isabella   110
   Lombarda   114
   Castelloza   118
   Clara d'Anduza   130
   Bieiris de Romans   132
   Guillelma de Rosers   134
   Domna H.   138
   Alais, Iselda and Carenza   144
   Anonymous I   146
   Anonymous II   152
   Anonymous III   156

APPENDIX
   Biographies   160
   Manuscript Sources   161

FOOTNOTES   180
SELECTED READING LIST   188
INDEX   191

ACKNOWLEDGMENTS

This book was helped along its way by the encouragement of so many different people that I cannot think of it as something I have made alone. I assume responsibility for any errors; much of the inspiration must be traced to other sources.

Of these the very first are strangers: the many thousands of women who are the Women's Movement, to whom I owe my own awakening. Their struggle for identity and selfhood is behind this book and in between its lines.

In passing from the unknown to the known, there is room here to acknowledge only those who worked directly with me on the book. Many wonderful friends supported me less tangibly but equally importantly.

It was Joan Kelly-Gadol of Sarah Lawrence College and the City College of New York who took this project on as a conference course at Sarah Lawrence College in the fall of 1972 and who first suggested that it be a book; Jane Cooper who sharpened my ear and opened my eyes. I am indebted also to Professor Charles Camproux of the Université Paul Valéry in Montpellier for his meticulous and illuminating help with the translations over a period of many weeks in the spring and summer of 1975.

Additional thanks go to my parents and my sister Nina for their constant enthusiasm and perceptive comments; to Richard Ehrlich, Michael Marqusee, Allen Graubard and Ann Popkin for their helpful criticism; to M. René Nelli of Carcassonne for his generous correspondence; to Joan Ferrante of Columbia University for her kind reading of the first drafts of the translations; to Frederick Goldin of the Graduate School of the City University of New York for permission to quote extensively from his translations of the male troubadours; to Mme. Agnes de Gunzbourg, for her extended hospitality to me while I was at work in Paris.

And lastly to Electa Arenal, who was a primary resource.

The author would like to acknowledge the generous support of the Ludwig Vogelstein Foundation of New York City and the National Endowment for the Humanities.

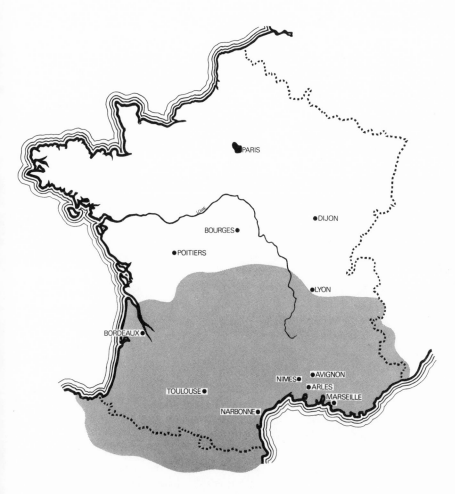

Present-day France showing approximate area of Occitania.

INTRODUCTION

LMOST EVERYONE has heard of the troubadours, the medieval singer-poets of the south of France. But hardly anyone, including specialists, is aware that there were women troubadours who lived and wrote in the same period – roughly the twelfth and thirteenth centuries – and the same area. Although eight of the women represented in this book are mentioned in the thirteenth-century *vidas* which are the major (if erratic) source of information on the troubadours, only a handful of them have been translated or studied. There have been articles here and there over the years about Azalais de Porcairages, Castelloza and the Countess of Dia, but these have been in scholarly reviews concerned with relatively technical aspects of the poems. The only study of the women troubadours *en masse* is a German monograph from 1888, to which I am indebted for the texts of all but two of the poems. However, at thirty-six pages *Die Provenzalischen Dichterinnen* can hardly be considered an exhaustive work. This book is the first full-length study on the women troubadours, as well as the first edition of their work to include translations.

Contrary to the popular image, most troubadours were not lute-strumming wanderers, but serious court poets who only rarely were forced to hawk their poems from castle to castle. They are perhaps best known to the general reader for their development of a set of amorous attitudes toward women which has come to be identified as courtly love. Beginning in the early years of the twelfth century, following the First Crusade, they were among the first to express what we might now call romantic love, as distinguished from, though not necessarily excluding, sexual passion. Their poems were addressed to women of the high nobility, to whom they vowed eternal homage and obedience. In exchange for their prostration, the troubadours expected to be ennobled, enriched, or simply made "better":

> *Each day I am a better man and purer*
> *for I serve the noblest lady in the world,*
> *and I worship her, I tell you this in the open.*

> *Arnaut Daniel*
> *fl. 1180–1200*

In almost every sense this poetry was new. For while the troubadours – the word means literally "finder," "inventor" – distilled their rhymes from older sources, they were among the earliest to elevate vernacular speech to the status of a literary language. They wrote in *lenga d'oc*, now generally called Provençal, a language that has more in common with Portuguese or Spanish than it does with modern French. This similarity has its roots in medieval history. France as we know it did not exist in the twelfth century; instead, there were a number of distinct and unaffiliated areas, most of which had their own languages and cultures. Two broad territories, roughly corresponding to the unequal sections north and south of the Loire river, can be distinguished. While the south spoke *lenga d'oc* (from which it took the name of Occitania), the northern tongue was known as *langue d'oïl* – *oc* and *oïl* (modern French *oui*) being the words for "yes" in the respective languages. Just as *lenga d'oc* and *langue d'oïl* were different enough to be mutually foreign, the two French cultures were worlds apart. Both geographically and culturally, the north was closer to England and the German-speaking countries; the south, which had been more thoroughly colonized by Rome, felt itself much closer to Italy and Spain.

The troubadours' use of *lenga d'oc* spurred the development of poetry in all the other nascent languages of Europe. By the beginning of the thirteenth century, imitations of the Provençal *chanson*, or love song, were being written in Italian, German, Spanish, *langue d'oïl* and even English. This medieval poetry produced a double legacy, which continues to determine a good portion of the Western world of feeling. Through Dante's Beatrice, love was proclaimed the supreme experience of life, and the quest for love, with the lady as its guiding spirit, became the major theme of Western literature. Long after the courts of southern France had become extinct, the intricacies of courtly conduct lived on in "civilized" society as chivalry, the obligatory deference to women as the weaker, purer, more virtuous sex.

The elevation of the lady in the poetry of courtly love was a distinct reversal of the actual social status of women in the Middle Ages, and there has never been agreement among scholars as to just how seriously the troubadours meant their conceits of woman-worship. Throughout the Middle Ages women were the pawns of men. Depending on their class, they lived in varying degrees of comfort or misery. Only in the most exceptional cases did they have any say in their own destiny. Marriage was a creation of the aristocracy, an economic and political contract designed to solidify alliances and guarantee the holdings of the great land-owning families. Following the rise of commerce, it was adopted by the bourgeoisie for these same reasons – as a means of maintaining and advancing their economic and political status. Alliances among the mass of laboring peasants, who had no stake in either property or commerce, were generally informal; marriage was only relevant where there were interests to be handed down to a new generation. Love or affection had little to do with the making of marriages. The woman was a breeder of sons, and her success in this one

function was the measure of her usefulness. If she failed repeat-
edly – either by being sterile or by conceiving endless daughters
– she was repudiated and sent home to her parents or placed in
a convent. She had no legal recourse, nor was she allowed to
dangle husbandless for very long: repudiation was followed by
remarriage as soon as an appropriate husband could be found.
The Church regarded women as so many incarnations of Eve,
"the first sinner." St. Jerome, the arch-misogynist of all time,
considered woman "the gate of the devil, the patron of wicked-
ness, the sting of the serpent." Procreation was a necessary evil;
marriage was accepted only with reluctance: "Better to marry
than to burn." For the Church Fathers, virginity alone could
truly detoxify the female sex. The doctrine of Immaculate Conception, which made the Virgin Mary herself the child of a
virgin birth, was an ingenious way of sparing Jesus Christ the
indignation of having to pass through a contaminated mother.
As a second generation virgin, Mary presumably was free of the
curse of Eve. This was the context in which the poetry of courtly
love appeared. Although many theories have been advanced,
there has never been a satisfactory explanation of what made
the troubadours begin to praise the lady in a time of such
widespread misogyny.

The poems of the women troubadours are therefore of the
utmost interest. Some of the *trobairitz*, as they were called in
Provençal, belong among the finest voices of the courtly lyric.
They are also the first female witnesses we have – and perhaps
the only ones whose testimony has survived – from a culture
that has profoundly influenced our own and which has hitherto
been represented only by its men. There were twenty known
women troubadours, eighteen of whom are represented in this
book.§ Since manuscript survival depends so much on chance,

§ There are no extant poems by Gaudairença, whose name is given
in the *vidas* as the wife of the troubadour Raimon de Miraval.
A long religious poem by Gormonda de Montpellier, a line-by-line
refutation of an anti-Vatican attack by the troubadour Guillem
Figueira, is of interest only for Church history.

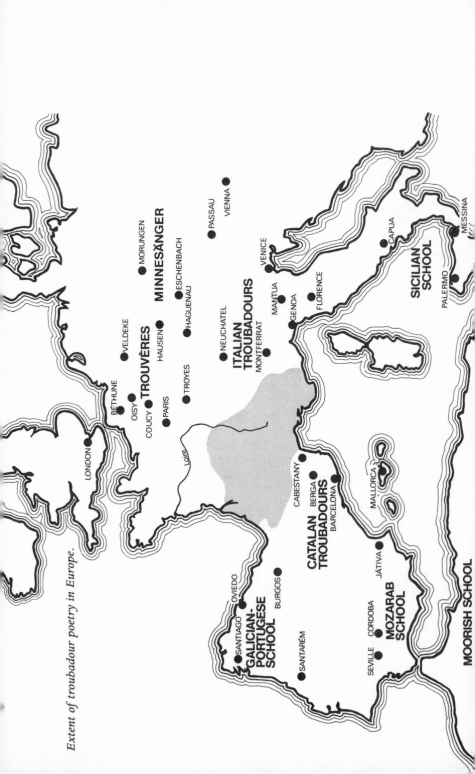

Extent of troubadour poetry in Europe.

there is every reason to believe that there were more. Moreover, since the *vidas* show that almost half of the *trobairitz* were known as poets in their own lifetimes, it is likely that the extant work (only two of them have more than one poem to their name) represents only a fragment of their actual output. Nonetheless, the twenty-three poems that have survived challenge our assumptions about the world in which the courtly lyric first arose.

To begin with, their very existence requires explanation. Women poets in the Middle Ages are practically unheard of, and to find twenty of them living in one small area and within the brief span of a century is cause for some astonishment. Despite the rapid spread of troubadour poetry to all the neighboring communities (see map, p. 12), Occitania alone – the cradle of the courtly lyric – produced women troubadours.

Secondly, although they wrote about love, the women's language and the situations they describe are strikingly different from those of their male counterparts. Their verse is rhymed, but there is less word play and less interest in the exercise of craft than in the men's poems; the women prefer the more straight-forward speech of conversation. Perhaps this is because the women, unlike the men, do not idealize the relationships they write about, nor do they use the lover and the lady as allegorical figures. The women write about relationships that are immediately recognizable to us; they do not worship men, nor do they seem to want to be adored themselves.

What was it about twelfth-century Occitania that permitted such a flourishing of women poets? Was there a connection between the women troubadours and the rise of courtly love? If the poems of the *trobairitz* are different from the men's, what do they have in common with each other? These initial questions led me in three main directions, which are represented by the three divisions of the essay.

In the first part, "Historical Background," I attempt to account for the existence of the women troubadours by looking at the history of southern France in the period leading up to the

Crusades. Since my research showed that the women troubadours were all aristocrats, this section concentrates on changes in inheritance law, which were relevant only for the small group of propertied women to which the women troubadours belonged. There were substantial differences in the legal status of aristocratic women in the south of France and elsewhere in Europe, including northern France. Special attention is also given to the rise of commerce and the effects of the Crusades, which significantly and rapidly developed Occitania in the early years of the twelfth century. It is no coincidence that the largest number of the women troubadours were from the valley of the Rhône, where the transformation had been most dramatic.

"Courtly Love: A New Interpretation" is the result of a series of speculations. The question of sincerity is perhaps a bogus one, but it is inevitable in the discussion of a poetry for which so much has been traditionally claimed. Several writers have regarded courtly love as a proto-feminist development, "an essential stage in the emancipation of women."[1] Because the lady of the troubadours had the power to accept or reject their love at whim, and because she had to be obeyed no matter how absurd her commands might be, it has even been suggested that women's unspoken desire for emancipation was the motive force of courtly love.[2] For C. S. Lewis, the troubadours "effected a change which has left no corner of our ethics, our imagination, or our daily life untouched, and they erected impassible barriers between us and the classical past or the Oriental present. Compared with this revolution the Renaissance is a mere ripple on the surface of literature."[3] The veneration of the lady was indeed a break with both the classical and early Christian traditions, both of which, from different points of view, had tended to view woman as a drastically inferior species. Courtly love was a radical change from both these attitudes in that it made women – always in the person of the lady – an integral part of culture. Yet almost two centuries ago, in her *Vindication of the Rights of Woman* (1792), the Englishwoman Mary Wollstonecraft questioned the extent to which the legacy of courtly love had benefited women:

"While they have been stripped of the virtues that should clothe humanity, they have been decked with artificial graces that enable them to exercise a short-lived tyranny." These contradictory views are mirrored in the contrast between the poetry of the male and female troubadours.

If, as the poems of the women troubadours seem to be saying, the men were hypocrites whose actions bore no resemblance to their words, then what was courtly love really about? If it was not meant as a serious code of conduct, was it simply a literary game? A philosophical allegory? What needs was it meant to satisfy? Were they the needs of men or women, both or neither?

While it is somewhat inexact to speak of a code of love – the troubadours never went so far as to produce an actual rule book§ – the poems of the 400-odd male troubadours contain a number of recurring themes. Humiliation to the lady, love as a means of spiritual improvement, the exclusive focus on married women of superior rank – these are the essential ingredients of the courtly lyric. The troubadours themselves had a single term for the ensemble of emotions and behavior they sang about: they called it *fin' amors*, literally "fine love." Within the long line of major troubadours, individual poets expressed themselves with great originality and talent, and with varying consistency about the kind of love they hoped for. For the purposes of this essay, however, I have focused on the central themes they shared rather than their differences, which have been well studied elsewhere.[4]

In tracing the development of courtly love through such master poets as Guilhem de Poitou, Bernart de Ventadorn, Peire Vidal and Peire Cardenal, we see the lady of the troubadours grow more and more ethereal until, in her Italian incarnation, she is immortal. In all these forms she faithfully reflects success-

---

§ *The Art of Courtly Love* by the monk Andreas Capellanus has traditionally been viewed as the only codification of the courtly love conventions. Recently there has been some debate about whether Capellanus' meticulous classification, written in 1184 in the manner of Scholastic argument, is serious or tongue-in-cheek.

ive changes in the needs of men. Beatrice may have been Dante's prime mover, but her actions were remote-controlled by him. Unfortunately, the effects of this poetic evolution were not confined within a literary universe. Desexed and beatified (Beatrice), definitively changed into man's spiritual redeemer, the lady of the poets became the mannequin with which all women were compared. Perhaps the elevation of the lady was a major turning point in the history of men; to consider this development a positive one for women would be to ignore its crippling effect on the women of succeeding centuries, including our own.

The section on courtly love provides the background for the third part of the essay, which is an introduction to the poetry of the women troubadours. The women's poems are written in two different forms, both of which were the main forms of troubadour poetry in general (although the men explored satiric verse in a form called the *sirventes*, which the women did not use). The *chanson* was a solo love song and was considered the highest expression of Provençal love poetry. The *tenson*, a more popular form, may have been performed before an audience, as improvised entertainment. It was generally a discussion between two people about the fine points of courtly behavior, although theoretically almost anything could be discussed. The two partners composed alternating stanzas which followed a consistent rhyme scheme. Most of the *tensons* in this collection are between a woman and a man; two are between two women.

Unfortunately, almost nothing is known about how these poems were composed. (For the male poets, too, this is an area where information is lacking.) There is evidence to indicate that the women troubadours could have been literate,[5] but whether or not it was customary for troubadours to write their poems down is still not known. Nor is it known whether the women actually performed their poems. Most troubadours of the nobility were able to afford the services of a *joglar*, a court performer (the word comes from the Latin *joculator*, juggler) who did the singing and embellished the musical composition. The poem of Azalais de Porcairages makes reference to a *joglar* in the *tornada*,

"A chantar m'er de so qu'ieu no volria," *by the Countess of Dia. Music and text (a variant of that included in the present volume) from a 13th-century manuscript.*
Bibliothèque Nationale, *Ms. FR. 844, fol. 204R.*

BOTTOM: *Juggler and musician. Codex of Latin hymns from the Church of St. Martial, Limoges. Late 10th century.*
Bibliothèque Nationale, *Ms. LAT. 1118, fol. 112V.*

or *envoi*, at the end. Some of the poems, however, including Azalais', are so personal that it is difficult to imagine that they were sung before an audience. The music for only one of the women's poems, "*A chantar m'er de so que no volria,*" by the Countess of Dia, has survived. This song can be heard on the record recommended in the Selected Reading List.

This book comes into being at a time when women everywhere, not for the first time in history but with a new historical consciousness, are re-examining the past in order to situate themselves more authentically in the present. In this context the poems of the women troubadours raise important questions which deserve to be taken up more fully elsewhere. How, for example, can we account for the women's unanimous rejection of symbolic love? Why do the women troubadours use so few images? Do women innately tend toward the concrete, men toward the abstract? The poems of the male troubadours have been considered part of a universal artistic heritage, but in the light of the women's poems, we see that they reflect a male view of relations between men and women.

Although the impetus has come from women, men too are beginning to analyze the ways in which their attitudes, both toward women and toward themselves as men, are controlled by myth and rooted in a particular historical development. Certain categories of thought before taken for granted as fixed and eternal – and natural – are now being looked at with a more critical eye (an eye, as Simone de Beauvoir puts it, which has long suffered from a blind spot over just that point where the relations between men and women pass before it).[6] Romantic love – love as perpetual torment, as ennobling force, as obstacle course (making its way around barriers of distance, class and marriage) – is one of the most deeply cherished ideals of the West. It is so much a part of our culture that it almost seems biologically determined. Romantic love may well be one of life's highest experiences, but because it is also the cause of great unhappiness for many people, there is reason to examine some of our prevailing attitudes – even if only in the end to reaffirm our faith.

The troubadours of southern France had more to do than is generally realized with setting in motion our present images of male and female, love and passion. Thus, my point in writing this book is not simply to unearth what by now cannot help being seen as a literary curiosity – women troubadours, imagine! – but to put forth a whole new set of questions, ones which arise from this particular set of poems, but whose frame of reference is much broader.

Except where otherwise indicated, all of the poems by male troubadours are translated by Frederick Goldin.

HISTORICAL BACKGROUND

U NLIKE SO many later women writers who were forced to hide behind men's names, the women troubadours wrote *as* women, and their poetry reveals a whole dimension of the Middle Ages that has for the most part gone unchronicled. But to understand their poems, and to account for their existence in an age of virulent misogyny, we need to take a sprinting look at medieval history, with a special interest in the role of women. This will also bring the background of the troubadours more clearly into focus.

The feudal hierarchy of medieval Europe was an intensely masculine system, based on military prowess and designed to safeguard the interests of individual men, or of individual men and their sons. In the early centuries A.D., in the aftermath of the first wave of "barbarian" assaults – Cimbrians, Allemans, Goths, Franks, Huns and Vandals *inter alios* – there had been a gradual breakdown of Roman legal and social patterns. Feudalism developed as a structure for mutual defense in the shaky period that followed these invasions, somewhere around the end of the sixth century and the beginning of the seventh. The Merovingian rulers of northern France – the crossroads *par excellence* of Roman and Germanic culture – had all they could do to keep a bit of peace. It was under their rather groping rule that feudal custom first took shape, and under Charlemagne, their successor, that custom became law and institution.

Feudal society can be described as consisting of two classes, lords and serfs. But within the group of lords – the old Roman aristocracy – there were the powerful and the less powerful. The key element in the hierarchy was the vassal, a man whose livelihood was guaranteed against a standing promise to defend another man, his lord, in time of war. The vassal's living was insured by grants of land, called *benefices*, worked by a whole community of serfs (whose own status as free men did not receive its full articulation until after the tenth century, with the arrival of true slaves, Slavic prisoners of war). In Celtic times, vassals had been free-lance warriors; under feudalism every man became a vassal. The men at the top, who held their land in *benefice* directly from the king, had vassals of their own, known as *chevaliers* (from Latin *caballus*, horse) or knights, who had vassals of *their* own, in a chain of service moving downward to the serfs. In this way, every member of society (males only) was tightly linked into a vertical seam of mutual obligation.

Everyone, even the most powerful lord, was required to perform the ritual of vassalage, or homage (from *homme*, liege-man), by which his lifelong loyalty to his immediate superior was sworn and sanctified. The future vassal knelt before his lord, hands joined; the lord placed his own hands around the clasped hands of the vassal. Then the vassal rose and, with his hand upon a Bible or some sainted relic, swore his oath of fealty. This simple ceremony would provide the central metaphor of troubadour love poetry, the vassalage of man to woman:

(Domna, per vostr' amor   *Lady, for your love*
jonh las mas et ador!)   *I join my hands and worship!*

                                        Bernart de Ventadorn
                                        fl. 1150–1180

In the warrior culture of the early Middle Ages (sixth through tenth centuries) women were virtual nonentities who counted only insofar as they were good for bringing sons into the world. If a young wife (marriage at twelve to fourteen was the norm) failed to produce an heir after a reasonable length of time, she was returned to her family, and the bride payment was refunded to her husband. Dowries, payments by the families of girls to their prospective husbands, did not appear until somewhat later, when the revival of Roman law allowed women to transmit, if not to own outright, the property of their paternal lineage.[1]

However, it is widely accepted that the laws and customs of the Mediterranean south of present-day France, the old *Gallia Togata* (Roman Gaul), were more favorable to women than those prevailing elsewhere in Europe. Two late Roman codices which took hold in that region in the sixth and seventh centuries were probably responsible, along with vestiges of certain Celtic and Visigothic practices,[2] for the relatively privileged status of Occitanian women in later centuries. Certainly the women troubadours, whose lives spanned the period between approximately 1150 and 1250, can be regarded as the beneficiaries of these early laws.

The Code of Justinian, compiled between 528 and 533 under the certain influence of the emperor's wife, the mime Theodora, reduced the husband's right to his wife's dowry to that of *usufructus*, meaning that he could use her land, but not claim ownership or pass it on to his own heirs.§ This important change gave women their first opportunity to exercise political control. In a culture where land was the chief source of power, the disposition and delegation of property was by definition a political act. However, despite their new right to inherit and, in a limited sense, to own, few women dared at this early date to challenge the prevailing notions of inheritance. Custom largely dictated

§ Salic law, which prevailed in northern France and England, prevented women from inheriting except when males were unavailable. In such cases, their property became their husband's when they married, along with the right to pass it on.

that property should go to sons in order of age, and only then to daughters. Much later, in 1171, Beatrix de Montpellier, an only child and heiress to the county of Montpellier, disinherited her son in favor of her granddaughter and daughter; even then such an action was probably exceptional.[3]

The Theodosian Code of 394–95, named after Theodosius, the Roman emperor who made Christianity a state religion, was brought to Occitania by the Visigoth invaders of the sixth century. This code gave sons and unmarried daughters an equal share in their father's estate. The customs of Montpellier state the principle quite clearly in the case of a father dying *ses gazi* – without a will: "the property of the father shall be divided equally between his son and his unmarried or undowered daughter" (*li ben del payre tornon al filh et a la filha non maridada ni heretada, per egals parts*).[4] While it is clear from Occitanian wills that this rule did little to disrupt the established preference for male heirs, it should not be overlooked as an important factor "on the books," the impact of which must be measured in a combination of historical shifts.

By the beginning of the tenth century, for example, a number of southern fiefs were in the hands of women, including the counties of Auvergne, Béziers, Carcassonne, Limousin, Montpellier, Nîmes, Périgord and Toulouse.[5] The granting of fiefs to women represented a fundamental threat to the feudal equation: military strength=land=power. A woman was not taught to duel, nor was she thought capable (like the *chevaliers*) of defending herself on horseback, a realistic skill for any fief-holder in those precarious times. Just why this central principle of feudalism was allowed in Occitania to be diluted by female inheritance has not been satisfactorily explained. Perhaps, as has been well argued, the racial and religious mixture of the south and, later on, the important maritime role of cities such as Aigues-Mortes and Marseilles, made Occitanians more tolerant and gave them greater flexibility of character.[6] Perhaps, on the other hand, the instances of women holding fiefs were so many "mistakes" on the part of individual families, which only over time appeared to constitute a valid legal principle for which the Theodisian Code was then invoked as model.

Certainly the Occitanians did not consciously set out to favorably alter women's status. Nor should the legal advantages enjoyed by Occitanian women (and only aristocrats) be interpreted with unwarranted enthusiasm. Their relatively privileged status in the early Middle Ages has more significance in retrospect than it had for them during their lifetimes. It was not until the early years of the twelfth century, under the impact of the First Crusade, that their descendants would begin to benefit from this legal inheritance. But for the moment we are in the early decades of the tenth, almost 200 years before the First Crusade.

The very fact that there is such a paucity of information on women of this period is, while not conclusive, an indication of their low position. Women of all ranks, even those who held property, were wards throughout the Middle Ages, always under the official guardianship of a man. The woman who inherited a fief, for example, was a mere stand-in for her husband, who actually controlled it. Only rarely were women permitted to appear in their own defense before a legal tribunal. In Germany, where they were allowed to do so, "the identical testimony of two or three women was supposed to equal the declarations of a single man."[7] In any case, legal rights and social attitudes were often, as now, at appalling variance.

The fact that women could inherit property, for example, in no way made them "masters" of their fate. Eleanor of Aquitaine was literally in danger of being kidnapped when she came into the vast inheritance of Aquitaine in 1132; it was only her extraordinary character (combined with her extraordinary rank) that made it possible for her to ditch one husband (the King of France) and select another (the King of England) in the style of the wife-repudiators of her time. More ordinary women had no say in whom they wed: among the aristocracy, and later on the bourgeoisie, marriages were generally contracted when the future spouses were in infancy, and girls were married in their early teens. If a man died intestate leaving an unmarried heiress, his lord could marry her himself (thereby annexing the dead man's fief) or choose her husband; a dying man would therefore take great care to specify his wishes for his daughter's marriage, as well as set aside a solid sum for her dowry. The risk if he didn't was too great: another man's choice, possibly an enemy's, might be imposed.

Peasant women were under the twin wardship of their guardian – whether husband or father – and their lord. The marriages of serfs were rigidly controlled; there were taxes for marrying, and special permission had to be requested for marrying outside a fief. But the worst expression of the peasant woman's exploitation was the *ius primae noctis*, the lord's right to his serf's bride on her wedding night. This practice was widespread throughout Europe, and continued well into the fifteenth century.[8]

Nor was class, however, a defense from rape. The crowded castles of the aristocracy gave noble women little privacy, and in the constant flow of guests and strangers apparently no one would think twice if a man was deft enough to catch some time alone with the lady of the castle. Even after later generations introduced more "courtly" conduct – restricting men, at least in theory, to raping women of the lower classes§ – women of the Middle Ages had no guarantee that they would not be raped in their own houses. One of the early records of the Inquisition, from Toulouse, tells of a noblewoman who was raped in her own bed while her husband had gone out to check the horses. She reports to the Inquisitors that she had never told him because she was afraid that he would throw the blame on her.[9]

---

§ "If you should, by some chance, fall in love with a peasant woman, be careful to puff her up with lots of praise and then, when you find a convenient place, do not hesitate to take what you seek and embrace her by force."

(Andreas Capellanus, *The Art of Courtly Love*, written in 1184)

BEGINNING AT THE end of the tenth century a number of important shifts set the stage for the Crusades and the poetic flowering of the twelfth century. While none of these changes was meant to alter women's status one way or another, the gradual awakening of European life, particularly in Occitania where the transformation was most rapid, brought currents that were positive for women.

Better agricultural techniques increased the food supply, and there was a sharp upward turn in population. Between approximately 1000 and 1300 Europe's population is said to have increased twofold.[10] For centuries vast inland areas had remained uncultivated and unexplored. Now the need for land became so pressing that a vast enterprise of clearing was begun, from Flanders to the Rhineland to the valley of the Po, and down into Occitania. In France the conquest of the hinterlands was aided by monastic orders such as the Cistercians, who would settle only on the most unpromising terrain. Also instrumental in the settling process were the Benedictines, who often stipulated that a town, or *bourg*, should be constructed to support the churches and abbeys that were going up in previously uninhabited places. The eleventh century was the great monastic century. In Occitania some of the outstanding structures from this period are St. Martin du Canigou (in the Pyrennees), Ste. Foi de Conques (in the Auvergne), the Abbey of St. Pierre at Moissac, north of Toulouse, and St. Guilhem-le-Désert, not far from Montpellier.

Abbaye de Sénanque, Gordes (Vaucluse). 12th-century cloister.
Héliogravure Lescuyer, Lyon.

The Cistercian Abbaye de Sénanque, near Avignon, built slightly later, is shown on p. 27. The creation and the growth of towns brought about the reawakening of the old Roman cities of the south. Nîmes (the Roman colony of Nemausus), Narbonne and Toulouse became the centres of the new culture that was forming.

The great Italian trading cities, Venice pre-eminent among them, had always sent a constant flow of goods to the Levant in exchange for the prized silks and spices of the East. But now, with Europe cleared and inland trade routes opened up along the rivers, commerce on a genuinely organized scale was possible for the first time. Increased trade stimulated cloth production in the towns of Flanders, where merchants from all over Europe flocked to trade. The wool of England, Spain and Scotland was the raw material for Flemish weavers; Lombard buyers took the finished cloth back down the Rhône through Occitania to Italy for shipping to the East. (Later, competition between Venice, Genoa and Pisa would give the Occitanian ports a heightened role.) On their way they might stop to trade at Avignon, Beaucaire or St. Gilles, which grew in time to rival the great fair towns of Champagne.

Added to the new commercial traffic were the throngs of pilgrims who began to crisscross Europe, particularly the south of France, on their way to Rome or Santiago de Compostela, in northwestern Spain. They too advanced the cause of commerce: they had to be fed and housed along their way, and were a constant market for the traveling salesmen of the Middle Ages. It is estimated that 500,000 people traveled the pilgrimage routes every year when pilgrimages were at their height.[11]

The renewal of commerce brought two related changes: a move away from barter in favor of a cash, or coin, economy; and the rise of a new class of people whose life was in the towns and whose status was derived from monetary wealth instead of land. The old feudal nobility found its base of power gradually eroded as the *nouveaux riches* began to buy up land. Land sale was profitable, and if the nobles wanted the exotic goods sold in the marketplaces of the *bourgs*, they had to learn a new equation: land = money = power.

The rise of the bourgeoisie created a new set of values, of the most important of which was a rudimentary notion of equality and citizenship: "Freedom became the legal status of the bourgeoisie, so much so that it was no longer a personal privilege only, but a territorial one, inherent in urban soil just as serfdom was in manorial soil."[12] In an atmosphere where escaped serfs became free men if they managed to remain within a city's walls for one year and a day (*Stadhoft macht frei*, according to the German proverb), it is likely that women also benefited, although evidence on this point is lacking. But it was not until the First Crusade, which galvanized the energies of every *bourg* and town, that women's lives would undergo dramatic change.

Thousands of people responded to the Pope's call in 1095 for a Christian army to retake Jerusalem from the Moslem "Infidel": the Crusades became one of the great mass movements history has known. A number of factors were important in drawing such a profound response, not the least of which was the extraordinary religious feeling of the Middle Ages. A pilgrimage to Jerusalem, as the Crusade was first described, was regarded as the ultimate expression of Christian faith. But religious zeal alone would not have moved such hordes of men (and some women) to undertake a voyage so exhausting and so hazardous as the journey to Jerusalem.

It is no coincidence that the greatest number of Crusaders came from Flanders and the Ile-de-France, the most densely populated areas of Europe.[13] In these areas, thousands of young men were more or less without a future. By making fiefs hereditary, feudalism had created its own undoing, for there was no principle of inheritance that worked to everybody's satisfaction. When primogeniture was followed to the letter, passing an entire fief to the first-born son, younger sons were left with nothing and could constitute a dangerous group of angry, often vengeful men. On the other hand, if their demands for land were met, and a fief was carved up into equal portions for however many sons there were, the size of the fiefs diminished rapidly over the course of a few generations, again creating discontent. While the south generally divided land in equal parts, Northern Europe tended to hold out for strict adherence to the principle of primogeniture. First-born sons inherited their father's land and title, second-born sons were sent into the Church, and any others would be out of luck unless they came from the most patrician families. For men such as these the Crusade stood for adventure and the possibility of gaining land and settling in the East. They had little to lose and everything to gain by going.

Other Crusaders were probably enticed by the excitement of combat. The knightly class was trained to fight, and regarded war as an activity midway between a sport and a duty or prerogative of their class (and sex). The troubadour Bertran de Born, writing in the second half of the twelfth century, made his reputation through magnificent poems glorifying war:

> Maces and swords and painted helms,
> the useless shields cut through,
> we shall see as the fighting starts,
> and many vassals together striking,
> and wandering wildly,
> the unreined horses of the wounded and dead.
> And once entered into battle
> let every man proud of his birth
> think only of breaking arms and heads,
> for a man is worth more dead than alive and beaten.[14]

It should not be forgotten either that the Crusades were highly profitable. In a feudal economy warfare was the vassal's only way of gaining land, and many of the men who took part in the first siege of Jerusalem were in fact rewarded with substantial pieces of the East. At the same time, the Crusades were one of the first large-scale adventures of the bourgeoning capitalist economy. The need for arms and all the paraphernalia of medieval war spurred the work of artisans such as the shield-maker troubadour Elias Cairel (see p. 111). The transport and housing of such unprecedented numbers brought windfalls to the shipping companies of Bari and the other ports used as connections to the

Knights in battle, from a 13th-century manuscript.
Bibliothèque Nationale, *Ms. FR. 15104, fol. 66V.*

Knights in Battle, from a 14th-century manuscript.
Bibliothèque Nationale, *Ms. FR. 10132, fol. 372R.*

Holy Land, as well as to the inns and hostels that sprang up all over Europe to accommodate the travelers.

Finally, there was the lure of the unknown. Trade with the East had whetted the Western appetite for a variety of Eastern goods – mainly silks, spices, jewels and richly ornamented *objets d'art* – and there must have been a widespread wish to see at first hand the lands from which these luxuries were brought.

After a first grisly failure in the fall of 1096, in which thousands of Crusaders were hacked to pieces by the Nicean Turks, Pope Urban II decreed that henceforth no women, and no old people or children, could take part in the Crusades. The first contingent had been poorly screened; too few knights had taken up the Cross. In his *Gesta Dei per Francos*, a contemporary chronicler, Gilbert de Nogent, described the pitiful band whose faith had been turned into fanaticism by ecclesiastic propaganda:

> Nothing more touching than the sight of these pathetic Crusaders shoeing their cows as if they were horses and yoking them to two-wheeled wagons onto which they piled their baggage and their little children. At every castle, at every town they saw along the way, they would stop, stretch out their hands, and inquire whether this was not the great Jerusalem toward which everyone was headed.[15]

A month after the massacre of this ill-prepared and unarmed grass-roots group, a new wave, presumably all male, set out to wrest the Holy Land back from the Moslems. This time every effort had been made to recruit experienced men-at-arms, and experienced men-at-arms tended to be noble. Special dispensations were extended to the lords and knights who crossed themselves. During their absence, often as long as ten years, all their property would be placed under the protection of a bishop. They could not be charged for any crimes they had committed and any debts they might have left behind could not be collected. In addition to material incentives there were religious ones: they were automatically washed clean of sin, and there was special glory – some said a guaranteed place in heaven – for those who went as pilgrims to Jerusalem.

In retrospect it hardly matters that the Crusaders failed to win their stated goal (in 1244 Jerusalem was back in Moslem hands and the last Christian fortress, at St. John of Acre, fell in 1291). This savage contact with the East brought Europe to its feet. The economic effects were probably the most dramatic: the influence of Arab art and architecture was immense. But the effect of the Crusades on women was equally profound and has been far less studied.

The troubadour Marcabru, in a remarkable transformation of the *pastorela*, or shepherdess' song, imagined the feelings of a young woman living at the time of the Second Crusade:

> *Her eyes welled up beside the fountain,*
> *and she sighed from the depths of her heart.*
> *"Jesus," she said, "King of the world,*
> *because of You my grief increases,*
> *I am undone by your humiliation,§*
> *for the best men of this whole world*
> *are going off to serve you, that is your pleasure.*
>
> *. . . I do believe*
> *that God may pity me*
> *in this next world, time without end,*
> *like many other sinners,*
> *but here He wrests from me the one thing*
> *that made my joy increase. Nothing matters now,*
> *for he has gone so far away."*[16]

If contemporary records are to be believed, some 60,000 men took part in the first siege of Jerusalem in 1099. The next hundred years would bring four more Crusades: in 1146, 1189, 1204 and 1217. In fact, however, the eastward flow of men was virtually uninterrupted throughout the course of the twelfth century, the officially proclaimed Crusades being mere highpoints in what really amounted to an ongoing war. The loss of men in the disastrous Third Crusade (they were all disastrous, but the second and the third were considered to have been

---

§ The capture of Jerusalem in 1147.

*Grave relief of Gérard de Vaudémont,
dressed as a Crusader, and his wife.
Second half of the 12th century.
Nancy, Chapelle des Cordeliers.*
Bildarchiv Foto Marburg.

particularly so) was estimated at 500,000, quite likely an exaggerated number; "but even a tenth of this figure would represent a fearful drain on the strength of Western Christendom, whose resources in manpower were already small enough."[17]

The most immediate effect of the drastic reduction in the male population was to place women in direct control of fiefs that had previously been run by men. There are countless examples of women who governed in their husband's name or were made regent, depending on the status of the husband. In Occitania in particular women took the reins of power. Phillipia, the wife of Guilhem de Poitou, the first troubadour, governed Aquitaine while he was in the East from 1101 to 1102.[18] The troubadour Almucs de Castelnau appears to have controlled Caseneuve while her husband was away. It seems likely that the north, more densely populated, was able to retain a firmer male control of property. Northern lords more often took their wives along with them (Urban II's all-male policy having gradually been relaxed) and left a near male relative in charge of their estates. Naturally there were northern women who stayed home and governed, just as there were Occitanian women who went on Crusade (the wife of Raimon IV of Toulouse had accompanied her husband on the First Crusade despite Pope Urban's ban). But whether they stayed home and kept things running, "thus performing an essential service for their families and for society,"[19] or whether they accompanied their husbands to the East, women's lives would never be the same: new worlds had opened up.

Up to this point women had been able to lead lives of relative autonomy only in the Church, an institution scarred by centuries of deep misogyny.[20] Woman-hatred did not disappear with the Crusades; in fact, under the aegis of Pope Gregory VII, who succeeded Urban II, there was a dramatic increase in the intensity of anti-female propaganda throughout the twelfth and thirteenth centuries, in an effort to persuade the priesthood to return to celibacy. This campaign was part of the Gregorian Reform, which was proclaimed in 1095, coinciding with the preaching of the First Crusade. It is therefore well to underscore the unintentional nature of the Crusades' positive effects on women:

> These ladies were almost by accident furnished with great power
> by a system devised for a society of a different character alto-
> gether . . . . As in the case of the lady abbess, feudalism played
> into the hands of the very persons to whose interests it was
> apparently inimical.[21]

If the effects of the Crusades on women were widespread and
profound throughout Europe and particularly in France, nowhere were they more explicitly registered than Occitania, in
the existence of the women troubadours. This is not the place
for a discussion of the conditions that allow an artist to arise,
which are particularly complex in the case of women artists. It is
clear, however, that the women troubadours belonged to a
uniquely favored generation. Certain key factors – their legal
heritage, the effects of the Crusades, and their aristocratic birth
– converged during their lifetime in a way that set them apart
from their mothers and grandmothers and from their contemporaries elsewhere in Europe. There was no comparable flourishing of women poets in any of the other areas where troubadour
poetry took hold (Marie de France, who wrote in northern
French, was virtually alone), nor had there been in Occitania
before the women troubadours nor was there after them.[22]

Yet the fact that a handful of aristocratic women wrote poetry
in Occitania in the twelfth and thirteenth centuries is not in and
of itself a clear-cut sign that the cause of woman had advanced:
it needs to be set into perspective. Before turning to the women
troubadours themselves – their lives and poems – we need to
get a sense of troubadour poetry in general and especially the
rise of woman-worship in the wake of the Crusades.

COURTLY LOVE:
A NEW INTERPRETATION

"To be in love is to stretch toward heaven through a woman."

Uc de St. Circ
13th-century troubadour

DIFFICULT AS it is to pinpoint the exact beginnings of artistic movements, the poetry of courtly love can be roughly traced to the early years of the twelfth century, the years immediately following the First Crusade. The Crusades had brought dramatic changes in almost every area of European life, no less in the realm of culture than in economics. The troubadours of southern France were part of a whole cultural awakening that has been likened to a "Renaissance of the twelfth century."[1]

The first known troubadour was an aristocrat, Guilhem de Poitou, whose songs were written to amuse the jaded noblemen who frequented his court in northern Occitania.[2] It is hardly likely that Guilhem set out to launch a whole new poetry, but it is undeniable that his poems caused a sensation among the friends and courtiers who rushed to imitate them.

Guilhem wrote about love in a way that was destined to give woman a new place in the imagination. In a neat reversal of his actual position in the feudal hierarchy (besides being the

seventh count of Poitiers he was also the ninth duke of Aquitaine),
he declared himself a servant and took a lady as his master.
Guilhem exalted this obedience to woman as the pathway to an
almost mystic joy:

> *No man has ever had the cunning to imagine*
> *what it is like, he will not find it in will or desire,*
> *in thought or meditation.*
> *Such joy cannot find its like:*
> *a man who tried to praise it justly*
> *would not come to the end of his praise in a year.*[3]

Such an attitude was novel indeed, coming from the head of a
powerful and influential court, and from a man also fond of
boasting of his sexual exploits. Of all the contradictory features
of his poems, the single strand most seized upon by his successors
was this attitude of homage to the lady, whom Guilhem had
called *midons*, "my lord":

> *Every joy must abase itself,*
> *and every might obey*
> *in the presence of Midons, for the sweetness of her welcome,*
> *for her beautiful and gentle look;*
> *and a man who wins to the joy of her love*
> *will live a hundred years.*
>
> *The joy of her can make the sick man well again,*
> *her wrath can make a well man die,*
> *. . . the courtliest man can become a churl,*
> *and any churl a courtly man . . .*[4]

Later poets used a single term to designate the set of feelings
that Guilhem had first expressed. They called it *fin' amors*,
literally "fine love" (as opposed to the lustier variety he had also
glorified), but more appropriately translated as courtly love.
For, despite its popularity and rapid spread to other parts of
Europe (see map, p. 12), the poetry of *fin' amors* retained throughout its course the stamp of its creation in the great halls of the
Occitanian courts.

Not long after Guilhem's death – he died a pilgrim at Santiago de Compostela in 1127 – troubadours were everywhere in Occitania. Over the course of the twelfth century, in the hands of a thicket of talented poets, Guilhem's conceits evolved into the complex code of love that later generations have called chivalry.

The knight's homage to his lady. Seal of Raymond de Mondragon.
Département des Médailles, Bibliothèque Nationale.

IN READING POETRY for its "message," as we will in the following pages, we need not be closed to the literary value of the
writing. It should be said that this is poetry that takes some get-
ting used to. On first reading it can seem quite flat; much, of
course, gets lost in the translation. Yet there is a richness and
variety to troubadour poetry which grows with each successive
reading. This is not the place to dwell on the more literary
aspects of the poems, but a few observations may be helpful in
advance of the quotations that illustrate this chapter.

In the Middle Ages architectural forms existed on a landscape
we have no way of restoring. While we seek impatiently for
something new, people of the twelfth and thirteenth centuries
may have known the different pleasure of return, or even that
of staying in one place and watching a cathedral change in
different light. When Azalais de Porcairages wanted to evoke
the city of Orange, it was in terms of architectural landmarks
that she sought the recognition of her hearers:

> To God I commend Bel Esgar
> and the city of Orange,
> and Gloriet' and the Caslar,
> and the Lord of all Provence,
> and all those there who wish me well,
> and the arch where the attacks are shown . . .[5]

The repetition of poetic forms may have functioned as another
kind of landmark to an audience that was primarily illiterate.
The troubadours zealously pursued all forms of repetition,
particularly rhyme; one of their most highly prized *trouvailles*
was the rhyming of a word with itself, which they called *rima
cara* (literally costly, or dear rhyme). The refrain *(refranh),*
common in some of the more popular song forms such as the *alba,*
or dawn song, and the *pastorela,* was another kind of repetition.
Perhaps a similar intention lies beneath the worn conceits of
Guilhem's heirs. Like any icon, the image needs to be immediately
recognizable. This is especially so in an oral tradition, which the
Provençal remained until it was picked up in Italy by Dante's
precursors.

As the poetic voice was passed from Guilhem to Marcabru and Cercamon, from Jaufré Rudel to Bernart de Ventadorn, Bertran de Born, Guiraut de Bornelh – to name only the stars – it grew more polished, more refined. There are those who accuse the later troubadours of lacking inspiration, and who find their even-handed mastery a sign of imminent decline; who miss in them the roughness and originality of Guilhem and Marcabru. It is true that for the most part the poems became increasingly conventional and formulistic as the century wore on; certainly in their lesser voices they were full of hackneyed (and hack) writing and clichés. But there was always room for great inventors: Raimbaut d'Orange and Arnaut Daniel are two prime examples. It is also important to remember that what we find tedious, already said, may have struck the medieval mind quite differently.

*Guiraut de Bornelh, from a 13th-
century manuscript.*
Bibliothèque Nationale, *Ms. FR.
12473, fol. 4R.*

FOLLOWING PAGE: *"And the arch where the attacks are shown."
Roman arch at Orange (Drôme).*
Archives Photographiques.

SCHOLARS HAVE BEEN arguing for centuries about the origins of courtly love, and it is likely that their musings will go merrily along their way for years to come. Basically, the matter hinges on whether courtly love was new or old, borrowed or invented.

Against the notion that courtly love heralds a revolutionary change in human sentiment it has been argued that Guilhem's themes were old as time; that ample evidence exists of poetry in Latin and in cultures up and down the map in which the love of men and women had been similarly celebrated long before the troubadours were born.[6] Still, interesting as it is to speculate about the universal aptitude for love, romantic or otherwise, the discussion of origins is useful only if it sheds some light on courtly love as it was practiced and expressed by the troubadours: that is, in Provençal, in southern France, beginning in the first years of the twelfth century.

For the fact remains that courtly love, whether or not it had had other incarnations in other languages and cultures, whether or not it was entirely new, was the moving spirit of a *new poetry*: the poetry of the troubadours of Occitania, who were among the first, if not the very first, to set about the conscious creation of a literary speech in the vernacular. *But why did they write so obsessively of women?*

It is not enough to say, as C. S. Lewis did, that the veneration of the lady was "natural":

> . . . Before the coming of courtly love the relation of vassal and lord, in all its intensity and warmth, already existed; it was a mold into which romantic passion would almost certainly be poured. And if the beloved were also the feudal superior the thing becomes entirely natural and inevitable.[7]

One of the special problems in writing about courtly love is that every historian is also a potential lover: "Nothing so moves a man's heart as the feeling of being submissive to a young and beautiful woman who permits him to breathe only in so far as she loves him."[8]

It has been suggested that the veneration of the lady (*la dompna*) was the expression of a deep psychological need left

A king of Aragon, from a 13th-century manuscript.
Bibliothèque Nationale, *Ms. FR. 854, fol. 108R.*

unmet by the unrelenting masculinity of feudal culture, the underlying premise being that a healthy society achieves a balance between "masculinity" and "femininity" and that the elevation of the lady was symbolic of the need for a corrective *feminization* of society. This kind of argument raises a number of questions. How do we *know* that there was such a need? And even if there was, how do we know that woman-worship was the answer, or the symbol? Again, without rejecting these ideas, it is important to be wary of carrying our own beliefs into our reading of the past. From our late twentieth-century vantage point we may well sense that something was not right in the feudal world of power and pillage – indeed, we had better. Nonetheless, we are not in a position to know whether the first troubadours (particularly Guilhem de Poitou with his bawdy stag songs) were as moved by their eulogies of women as some of their later readers.

On the other hand, there is a good deal to be said for the so-called Arab theory, which sees the courtly lyric of Provence as substantially derived, in both form and content, from the love poetry of Andalusia and Arabia, where Arab poets had been worshipping their ladies for at least 200 years.[9] René Nelli has shown that Guilhem's poems, rough-hewn as they are, contain the basic canon of ideas – homage to the lady, true love as endless suffering, chastity as the highest espression of true love – that Arab poets had already codified in works such as *The*

Dove's Neck Ring, a mid-eleventh-century treatise by the
Cordoban Ali ibn-Hazm, which contained a chapter on "The
Submissiveness the Lover Owes His Lady."[10]

Guilhem by all accounts did not begin to write until 1102,
just after his return from the Crusades. He had spent a year
semi-imprisoned at the court of Tancred, where, presumably,
he would have been exposed to Arab poetry.[11] Not only the
Crusades but the *Reconquista* – the continuing effort to reconquer
Spain from Islam – had created an important network of connections between Occitania and the resplendent courts of
Christian Spain, where Moorish poets and performers were in
residence. Spain was Occitania's closest neighbor, and there
was a constant flow of people back and forth across the Pyrennees.
Occitanian nobles often attended marriages in Castille and
Aragon; intermarriage between the ruling houses of Toulouse
and Barcelona would become a virtual chess-game in the late
twelfth century.

The influence of Arab culture was so pervasive that it was
hardly necessary to leave Occitania to hear the melodies of
Andalusia and Arabia. Much of southern France had been
conquered by Moslem invaders in the mid-eighth century.
Although the Saracens, as they were called, did not maintain their
hold for long, they left their mark in place names and, undoubtedly, in the folk imagination. Toward the end of the
eleventh century refugees from southern Spain began to settle
in the area of Nîmes and Montpellier, bringing Arabic and Arab
culture once again to Occitania. In Montpellier a colony of
Moslem refugees gave lessons in Moorish song and music; in
Narbonne, Béziers, Montpellier, Lunel and Vauvert, colonies
of Jewish translators and scholars, who were also Andalusian
refugees, taught Islamic and Hispano-Arab culture, including
poetry and music.[12] A slave trade in Moorish men and women
based in Narbonne began in 1149.[13] Inspired by their northern
counterparts, many Occitanian nobles kept troupes of Moorish
singers at their courts as a sign of status. Guilhem de Poitou
had himself grown up in the presence of hundreds of Moorish

joglaresas (female *joglars*) who were part of his father's court retinue: the elder count had won them in reward for helping Aragon campaign against the Moors in 1064.[14] The connections between Occitania and the Hispano-Arab world were so profound that, as Robert Briffault put it:

> There is no mystery about a process of difusion which ascertainable facts show to have been inevitable. What indeed would require a great deal of explaining is that any Provençal *jongleur* should have remained unacquainted with the lyric productions of Moorish Spain.[15]

It is impossible to know the exact degree and quality of Arab and Hispano-Arab influence on Guilhem and the other troubadours. For our purposes we can be satisfied with stating that there was considerable influence from both Spain and places further east, and that this accounts, at least in part, for the rise of courtly love poetry in Occitania on the heels of the Crusades and *Reconquista*.§ This conclusion raises another question. Why did these Arab-influenced ideas have such impact? Once imported, what gave them their extraordinary appeal? Initially, perhaps it was the sheer prestige attached to all things Eastern in the wake of the Crusades. But to understand the deeper causes, we will have to take a closer look at Occitanian society and the character of the courtly audience.

---

§ This is not to say that other forces did not enter in importantly – popular May songs, women's washing songs, Latin hymns to the Virgin, Latin love songs – but that the Arab influence was the single most important influence. The image of the lady in the courtly lyric was at once more sensual and more spiritual than anything that could have come directly from indigenous European sources.

Female joglar, or joglaresa. *St. Martial Codex. Late 10th century.*
Bibliothèque Nationale, *Ms LAT. 1118, fol. 114R.*

MOST OF THE troubadours who followed Guilhem IX were men of modest or even humble origins. Many of them were *joglars*-turned-poets; most depended for their living on the generosity of wealthy patrons. They were court poets, responsible for entertaining the large crowds that frequented the homes of Occitania's elite.

The model for their lady – the object of their eternal, abject passions – was the wife of their employer. If this sounds blunt it is nevertheless true, and it is in this light that all their bowing and scraping must, at least at first, be analyzed. As Maurice Valency put it, "most, if not all, of the troubadour poetry was written, as we say, on speculation, if not on assignment."[16] The wife of the *senhor* was rich and powerful. If her husband was away on military escapades or on Crusade, she was his replacement; even when he was at home it was often she who made cultural decisions.[17] She was the center of an overwhelmingly male court and, as the troubadours quickly discovered, the key element in the conflicting interests of the courtly population.

The courtly audience was not composed exclusively of nobles. Whether the artistocrats lived in the fortressed castles of the Occitanian hills or in the mansions of the newly thriving cities like Toulouse, their homes attracted a whole society of lower-ranking men who were in permanent, if precarious, residence. As Denys Hays describes it, "the knight or baron dwelt in . . . promiscuous intimacy with his household and retainers, rather like the captain of a small and overloaded ship on an uneasy sea."[18]

Within that shaky vessel, the troubadours had to please three different groups: the lord himself, upon whose grace they most directly counted, and his peers; his wife and her female attendants; and all the petty noblemen and court appendages, who were men of somewhat unclear status as feudalism started on its long decline. It was a difficult assignment, but by using words deliberately layered with multiple meanings, the troubadours were able to address all three at once.

In the case of a word like *midons*, for example, which they took up from Guilhem de Poitou, a single surface meaning could evoke a number of subsidiary meanings, each speaking to the aspirations of a different sector of the audience.§

> I love Midons and cherish her so much,
> fear her and attend to her so much,
> I have never dared to speak to her of myself,
> and I ask her for nothing, and I send her nothing.
> But she knows my sorrow and my pain,
> and when it pleases her, she gives me comfort and honors me,
> and when it pleases her, I make do with less,
> so that no blame should touch her.[19]

Bernart de Ventadorn
fl. 1150–1180

Linguistically, *midons* is a curious, almost hermaphroditic word: *mi* is probably a shortened form of the feminine possessive *mia* (the masculine was *meus* or *mos*), while *dons* is clearly masculine, deriving from the Latin *dominus*. This startling usage deserves more than the puzzled treatment it has usually received. What did this form of address imply? And to whom were the poets really talking?

First and foremost, *midons*, while not a proper name, served as a *senhal*, a code name which let everyone fill in his or her own details.[20] It was therefore an ingenious form of flattery. By refusing to disclose his lady's name, the troubadour permitted every woman in the audience, notably the patron's wife, to think that it was she; then, besides making her the object of a secret passion – it was *always* covert romance – by making her his lord he flashed her an aggrandized image of herself. She was more than "just" a woman: she was a man.

At the same time, by no small coincidence, *dons* expressed the troubadour's exact relation to his patron, who was indeed his lord; with the addition of the feminine possessive in *midons*, the poet's flattery remained appropriately oblique. Was he not perhaps praising the patron's wife – that wonderful, beautiful,

---

§ The Arab poets had used a similar form of address, variously given as *sidi* or *sayidd* – "my lord" – in their love poems to women.

pure and above all virtuous woman? She was perfection itself;
the patron had chosen wisely:

> *I cannot say anything bad about her, because nothing bad is in her –*
> *if I knew anything, I would tell it with joy,*
> *but I do not know one bad thing about her, and so I say nothing.*[21]

Bernart de Ventadorn

Thirdly, the atmosphere of secrecy and reverence drawn about
the figure of the lady by the ambiguity of *midons* permitted her
to correspond to no real person. For those truly in the know, the
troubadour was only pretending to be flattering the patron and
his wife, when he was in fact singing about something else
entirely: a new conception of nobility. *Midons* was generous,
midons was kind. She also had the quality of *merce*, not exactly
mercy or pity but a kind of discerning recognition of someone
lower than herself – always male – whose quality as a person
distinguished him from his fellows. But what was going on
beneath this sudden craving to be noticed? And beneath the
sudden penchant for humility on the part of men who only
decades earlier had been content with rougher pleasures?

Society's ground was shifting, and there was as yet no clearly
defined place for the restless offspring of the bourgeoisie, the
sons of former serfs or the landless sons of poverty-stricken
nobles. With his image of the noble lady deigning to receive the
low-born poet as her vassal, the troubadour extended to these
footloose men the possibility of membership in a new aristocracy,
an aristocracy based not on noble birth or feats at arms, but on
nobility of spirit.

It was in the name of these aspiring knights – the disinherited
of feudalism – that courtly love proclaimed itself a patrimony
any man could have if he was "courtly." The lady was the means
and inspiration to this new estate:

> *And if I can do or say a thing or two,*
> *let the thanks be hers, for she*
> *gave me the understanding and the craft,*
> *because of her I am courtly and a poet ....*[22]

Peire Vidal
fl. 1180–1205

Courtliness – *cortesia* – was his if she could accept him as her servant:

> *Good lady, I ask you for nothing*
> *but to take me for your servant,*
> *for I will serve you as my good lord,*
> *whatever wages come my way.*[23]

> Bernart de Ventadorn

Already Cercamon (fl. 1135–1145) had made love and courtliness synonymous:

> *Cercamon says: the man who gives up*
> *on love will never be courtly.*§

> *(Cercamon ditz: greu er cortes*
> *hom qui d'amor se desesper.)*

The later poets equated courtliness and *manliness*, putting war and woman-worship on an equal footing:

> *No matter what I do, I look like a knight,*
> *for I am a knight, and in love I am the master of the craft,*
> *and of everything that is proper when a man is with a woman;*
> *there never was a man so pleasing in a chamber*
> *or so savage and excellent in armor,*
> *and so I am loved and dreaded by such as do not even see me*
> *or hear my words.*[24]

> Peire Vidal

These lines of Bernart de Ventadorn, with their meshing of social and poetic logic, show how thoroughly the troubadours had come to represent the insecure, aspiring knights. If the poet lost his lady's love, he would find himself once more *sans héritage* and *sans métier*.

> *But, on the other hand, if I lose her friendship*
> *I hold myself disowned*
> *by love, and then God never let me*
> *write a* vers *or* canson *again.*[25]

The use of the word friendship (*amistat*) to describe the

---

§ Author's translation

troubadour's relation to his lady has led to interminable speculation. What kind of *amors* was this? Did they meet in the corridors?
Was it all in the mind? The poetry itself is so ambiguous, so
cautious, that almost anything can be read into it and indeed,
almost everything has.

> With the water I weep from my eyes
> I write more than a hundred love letters
> and send them to the most beautiful,
> the courtliest.
> Many times it reminds me afterwards
> of what she did when we parted:
> I saw her cover her face,
> so that she could not tell me yes or no.[26]

Bernart de Ventadorn

Some scholars have preferred to read this as platonic love,[27]
some have called it a cover for adultery,[28] others see it as
religious allegory.[29] There is no reason to throw out any of these
readings – they were probably all to varying degrees (along with
more we may not have thought of) intended to be there.

Mores in the south of France, at least among the aristocracy,
are said to have been more relaxed than elsewhere. The Gregorian
Reform, for example, did not succeed in Occitania in drawing
nuns and priests back into the fold of celibacy.[30] In courtly
society too, where large numbers of unmarried men lived under
one roof with a small number of mostly married women, and
where marriage was an economic and political arrangement,
there must have been enormous sexual tension. It is unlikely,
however, that adultery was as blithely practiced in the Occitanian courts as Robert Briffault would have us think.[31] There is
evidence, for example, that any man caught naked with his
patron's wife would have been in trouble.[32] For women,
adultery was more than sinful: it held the added risk of pregnancy. Besides the danger of childbirth the woman pregnant
through adultery faced possible repudiation, banishment (generally to a convent) or even – though perhaps not in Occitania –
death.[33] However, while sexual love could expose her to the

punishment of the Church and of society, in Occitania these same institutions seem to have tolerated deep affection without physical involvement. It is clear from the poems of a number of the women troubadours that love in this sense occupied a central place in their emotional lives. On the other hand, several of the women troubadours speak openly of scenes in bed. It is impossible to know whether to take their poems as evidence of actual practice. Given the social pressures against, it seems likely that courtly love, at least in theory, legitimated not adultery (as Briffault believed) but the fantasy of adultery. In practice, for both men and women, the forms love took probably depended on a combination of their needs, beliefs and circumstances, more than on a rigid code of love.

Yet the possibility of adultery inherent in the courtly setting does not explain the fact that only married women were the object of the troubadours' entreaties. Why were *donzelas* not equally desirable? Several central themes of courtly love may yield an answer.

One of the early and persistent concepts of the troubadours was that the lady's love enhanced the *value* of her lover. Value (*valors*) was a vague concept which must have played on its double sense of spiritual and financial worth – reflecting the growing importance of a cash economy – as well as drawing on its homonym, the knightly virtue of valor. According to the theory, both the lover and the lady had to have *valors*: she had it automatically through her husband, but the knight's could be increased, along with his *pretz* (merit), if he was the lover of a noble woman.[34] Thus, the man became apprenticed to the lady; through her he could be *enriched* – again, in the double sense:

> *If the beautiful lady I want to belong to*
> *wants to honor me*
> *just so much that she agrees to let*
> *me be her faithful lover,*
> *I am mighty and rich above all men.*[35]

> *Guiraut de Bornelh*
> *fl. 1165–after 1211*

The lady was a passive figure in this operation. There was never any mention of *her* gaining *valors, ricors* or *pretz*, since by definition she already had them. True, the troubadour's happiness depended on the lady's yes or no, but this apparent exercise of power on her part was virtually mechanical. It cannot be entirely a coincidence that the troubadours often called their ladies *res*, the word in Provençal and Latin for "thing":§

Sweet well-bred thing,
may He who fashioned you so nobly
grant me that joy I so await in you.†

(Dousa res ben ensenhada,
cel que.us a tan gen formada
me.n de cel joi qu'eu n'aten.)

However, returning to the use of "lord" (*midons*) to designate the lady, and remembering the social aspirations of the knights and court retainers, we can see in the lady a simple conduit of status.[36] This may be the key to the troubadours' exclusive interest in the *dompna*.

Only married women had irrevocable rank. The unwed woman belonged to her father's class, the married woman to her husband's. Thus, a woman who was still unmarried was a risk; she could go up or down, depending on her father's skill in marrying her off. On the other hand, since divorce did not exist (annulment was the privilege of a special few), the married woman was invested for life with the status of her husband.

The lowly knight seeking to enhance his lot could not approach the powerful *senhor* directly in the hopes that some nobility might rub off on him; his desire for upward mobility would by its very nature threaten the lord's power and virility. The lord's wife, however, was a convenient stand-in for her husband, as long as everything remained symbolic. The knight's humility,

---

§ The word *res* was also used to mean creature, matter, idea, reality, etc., but I am calling attention to its *literal* meaning.
† Author's translation

his "correct" attitude, was his passport to the lady's favor; her favor was the needed passport to her husband's. Her acceptance of the homage of the knight (troubadour) raised him to new heights:

> Every day I am a better man and purer,
> for I serve the noblest lady in the world,
> and I worship her, I tell you this in the open.[37]

Arnaut Daniel

Perhaps, as the sexual ambiguity of *midons* suggests, and despite the seeming adoration of the lady, the troubadours were really "courting" women to reach their men. The lady would thus be the mediator in a symbolic transference of status between two men of different social classes.[38] And courtly love, with its imagery of sexual flirtation, might therefore also be described as a coquetry of class.

Of course, the troubadours did not compose their poems with these ideas in mind. As far as they were concerned, they were talking about a genteel form of friendship between men and women (with an occasional titillating twist); their job was the elaboration of its rules in complex chains of rhyme. Yet it was their special genius to hit upon a language that voiced beneath its surface the deepest longings of their audience. By borrowing so extensively from the vocabulary of feudalism they grounded courtly love in a reality that had, even in Occitania, a powerful hold on the imagination of their public. And by constantly exploiting the ambiguity and multiplicity of meaning they made their poetry the vehicle of many messages. In this way, the sexual expressed the social and the social the sexual; and in the poetry of courtly love the static hierarchy of feudalism was uprooted and transformed to express a world of motion and transformation.

Thus, within the framework of the cult of woman, a whole new set of values was struggling to be born. The troubadours extended to their audience an intuition of equality and freedom that was unheard of in the Middle Ages. Yet it would be wrong to leap to the conclusion that this represented a momentous change for women. The women in the troubadours' immediate audience may have benefited from the songs sung in their honor (as we shall see in section 3), but courtly love was essentially a system men created with the dreams of men in mind. If women were among its most important patrons, it is principally because they stood to benefit from men's new "courtly" attitudes. Aristocratic women in Occitania had the power to support a movement that appeared to offer them prestige. But the degree to which the veneration of the lady was a veneration of the lady for *her* sake remains extremely questionable.

IN 1209 POPE Innocent III proclaimed a new Crusade: the target was Occitania. The Albigensian Crusade, as it came to be called, was ostensibly an attack on heresy; but when the French king threw his weight behind the effort, recruiting Northern barons to the cause, it fast became a war of annexation. A number òf heretical sects, most importantly the Waldensians and Albigensians (known also as Cathars), had been quietly gathering converts in the south of France during the preceding centuries. They were pacifists and vegetarians, and advocated a return to the pure Christianity of the early Church. Essentially, they followed the Gnostic belief in two opposing powers, Good and Evil. Spirit was good, flesh was evil; therefore they denied the Incarnation. They considered women and men equals; women converts to Catharism, in which women were allowed to preach, vastly outnumbered men.

The Pope provided powerful incentives to the Northern volunteers. He offered them the same rewards for taking up the cross in Occitania they would have had for going all the way to Palestine. For forty days' service their debts were lifted, their souls cleansed of sin and their place in heaven guaranteed. In addition, any land they conquered from the heretics was theirs to keep. Small wonder that all Occitania was quickly found to be heretical.

Within fifty years of Innocent's first call to arms, the great cities of the south would lie in ruins. Béziers, Carcassonne, Narbonne, Toulouse – all were overrun. Thousands of people were burned at the stake, killed in combat, stoned, raped. The last outpost of Cathar resistance, the Pyrennean fortress of Monségur (which has today become a symbol of Occitanian identity), fell in 1244. In the succeeding decades French language, law and custom were established in the south. The forced marriage of Occitanian heiresses with northern lords quickly brought the largest fiefs under French control. Women lost the rights that Occitanian law had guaranteed them. Primogeniture was rigidly enforced. The south of France never recovered from this virtual annihilation of its culture, although there is a marked nationalist sentiment in present Occitania, where Provençal, now known as Occitan, is still a spoken language.

Troubadour poetry was one of the first casualties of the Crusade. There is no agreement about just why the poetry was found subversive; it seems to have been taken as a symbol of the whole southern way of life which the north, and the Vatican, found so offensive. In any case, under the pressure of the Inquisition, which was created in Toulouse to interrogate Cathars, courtly love was found to be almost as heretical as heresy.[39] As early as 1209, Gui d'Ussel (whose *tenson* with Maria de Ventadorn appears on p. 98), was made to promise to a legate of the Pope that he would stop composing. Although the actual fighting took place in the area west of the Rhône, the effects were felt throughout the south, and many troubadours went into exile in Italy or Spain. Those who stayed fell silent or were forced to change their songs.

They still sang of adoration but the lady they adored had changed. The patron's wife had become the Virgin Mary. At first the switch to Mariolatry was barely audible: except for an occasional Maria, the language stayed extremely close to that of courtly love. Here, in the rhythms of the Latin church hymns, is Peire Cardenal's (1180–1278) song to the Virgin. The use of the word *amia* (friend, lover) is an example of the carry-

over from poems written to a less celestial lady. I have emphasized
the other words that seem to me to come from *fin' amors*:

Vera vergena, Maria,	*True virgin, Maria,*
vera vida, vera fes,	*true life, true faith,*
vera vertatz, vera via,	*true truth, true path,*
vera vertutz, vera res,	*true virtue, true* thing,
vera maire, ver' amia,	*true mother, true* friend *(lover),*
ver' amors, *vera* merces;	*true* love, *true* mercy:
per ta vera merce *cia*	*grant by your true* mercy
*qu'*eret *en me tos* heres!	*that your* heir inherit *me!*§

According to some scholars, the free spirit of the troubadours
was kept alive into the fourteenth century by the Franciscan
monks known as *Esperitals,* with whom Peire Cardenal appears
to have had ties. The cult of the virgin would therefore have
assumed enormous social and political significance.[40] There

---

§ Author's translation.

Carcassonne, showing 14th-century double ramparts.
Editions SL, Villeurbanne.

are ongoing discussions about whether many late poems composed to ladies are actually written to the virgin, and vice versa.

Be that as it may, it is most important that the adoration of the lady, whether as Our Lady or simply as *la dompna*, was able to survive the Albigensian Crusade and the virtual destruction of the Occitanian courts and of the men and women who had been the models for the characters of courtly love. The lady, far from being inessential to the ideology of *fin' amors*, was most essential. But she did not need to be real. She was a symbol, a cipher, an accessory. A brilliant life awaited her.

Dante and his contemporaries took her up intact and passed her on to the Rennaissance with the full bloom of Neo-Platonism on her cheeks. She was no longer *midons*, she was *Madonna*; she was no longer human, she was immortal.

> My lady is desired in highest heaven:
> now would I tell you of her excellence.
> . . . Love says of her: "How can a mortal thing
> be so adorned with beauty, and so pure?"§

> (Madonna è disiata in sommo cielo:
> or vòi di sua virtù farvi savere.
> . . . Dice di lei Amor: "Cosa mortale,
> come esser pò sì adorna e sì pura?")

Dante, Vita Nuova

OPPOSITE: *Monségur, last Cathar fortress (Ariège).*
Reportage Photographique YAN.

§ Author's translation.

Places of residence of the women troubadours.

Principal centres of troubadour culture in Occitania
⚑ : *Abbey.*

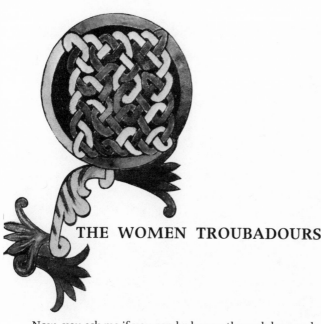

THE WOMEN TROUBADOURS

Now, you ask me if you can be happy through love and marriage.
I do not believe you will be happy through either, I am convinced
of it. But if you ask me in what other conditions the happiness
of women may be found I should tell you that as I am unable to
shatter and remold society entirely, and well knowing that it
will last beyond our own short sojourn here in this world, I must
place the happiness of women in a future in which I firmly believe,
in which we shall go back to better conditions in human life in
the bosom of a more enlightened society, in which our intentions
will be better understood and our dignity better established.

George Sand
Letter to Mlle. Leroyer de Chantepie
August 28, 1841

THE WOMAN troubadour is neither Dante's Beatrice
nor the Virgin Mary, the two key idealizations of
woman in the later Middle Ages. That there were
women troubadours is less surprising than we might
originally have thought. The *trobairitz,* as they were called in
Provençal, were the very ladies at whose skirts the troubadours
had knelt, the wives and daughters of the lords of Occitania.

Joglar *(left) entertaining a lady. 12th-century wooden marriage chest from the collection of the Louvre.*
Archives Photographiques.

There was no one to whom courtly love had spoken more directly.

There is little doubt that all of them knew male troubadours and lived among them. Tibors was a sister of the brilliant troubadour Raimbaut d'Orange; Maria de Ventadorn married into a long line of viscount-troubadours named Ebles.[1] Guillelma de Rosers, Alamanda and Isabella exchanged *tensons* with Lanfrancs Cigala, Guiraut de Bornelh and Elias Cairel, respectively. Almost a third of them at least – Clara d'Anduza, Almucs de Castelnau, Tibors, Maria and Garsenda – were patrons. Their lives spanned the full development of courtly poetry, from its first flourishing to its decline; and they lived in the centers where the art was practiced and refined.

They were thus in the unique position of being women in a world where women were officially adored. More accurately, they were the living, breathing model for *midons*. For whether they were patrons or simply members of the audience, as aristocratic women they were the inspiration and the object of the poets' reverence and praise. It was the first good word for women in a long time (and, as we have seen, it would be short-lived). Indeed, they were among the privileged few upon whose ears such flattery would fall for centuries to come.

With the benefit of time and distance we can say that they were not essential to the long-range purposes of courtly love. But whether courtly love ultimately had them in mind or not is more our concern than theirs. As they would probably have seen it, the ideology of *fin' amors* accorded women the prestige they deserved – and which life actually withheld. Perhaps they mistook flattery for admiration. But, as Emily James Putnam said in 1910, "it is certain that every lady who listened to troubadour or *jongleur* . . . was furnished with the material for constructing a fresh estimate of her own importance."[2] If *fin' amors* gave them the confidence to write, our scepticism should give way to gratitude. Their poems are gems.

Their most immediate appeal is their extraordinary freshness. They are as clear and candid as if they had been written down a day or two ago:

> *Elias Cairel, I want to know*
> *the truth about the love we two*
> *once had; so tell me, please,*
> *why you've given it to someone else . . .*

Isabella

and not at all what one might have feared from the presiding ladies of a formal world:

> *. . . nor did a time ever arrive, sweet handsome friend,*
> *when I didn't want to see you often;*
> *nor did I ever feel regret,*
> *nor did it ever come to pass, if you went off angry,*
> *that I felt joy until you had come back.*

Tibors

We are miles from *midons*. The voices of the women trouba-dours are as complicated as the voices of real people, and as earthbound. They sound like women any one of us could know. Unlike the men, who often wrote in the persona of the knight, the women wrote in no one's character but their own. And no two of them sound alike. Some are unhappy:

> . . . and if I'm sad and mournful
> it's because you don't remember me.
> And if still I have no joy from you
> you'll soon come upon me dead:
> for when unhappiness persists
> a woman dies, unless her man speeds joy.

Castelloza

ABOVE: *Countess of Dia, from a 13th-century manuscript.*
Bibliothèque Nationale, *Ms. FR. 854, fol. 141R.*

ABOVE RIGHT: *Man and Woman, from a 13th-century manuscript.*
Bibliothèque Nationale, *Ms. FR. 12473, fol. 22R.*

BOTTOM RIGHT: *Two lovers, from a 13th-century manuscript.*
Bibliothèque Nationale, *Ms. FR. 854, fol. 121V.*

Some are elegant:

> *Lady Almucs, with your permission*
> *let me request that in place*
> *of anger and bad grace*
> *you show a kinder disposition*
> *toward him who slowly dying lies*
> *lamenting amidst moans and sighs . . .*

Iseut de Capio

Some are blunt:

> *Elias Cairel, you're a phoney*
> *if I ever saw one,*
> *like a man who says he's sick*
> *when he hasn't got the slightest pain.*

Isabella

Some are proud:

> *I have a friend of great repute*
> *who towers above all other men,*
> *and his heart toward me is not un-*
> *true, for he offers me his love . . .*

Azalais de Porcairages

Some are hurt in love:

> *Of things I'd rather keep in silence I must sing:*
> *so bitter do I feel toward him*
> *whom I love more than anything . . .*

Countess of Dia

And some are happy:

> *If you knew my mind, sweet handsome friend,*
> *your handsome noble learned heart*
> *no longer would lament; for you're the one*
> *who's made me happier today than ever.*

Anonymous III

The language is direct, unambiguous and personal. Even where the technique is of the highest order, as in the poems of the Countess of Dia, the most striking aspect of the women's verse is its revelation of experience and emotion. Unlike the men, who created a complex poetic vision, the women wrote about their own intimate feelings. Sometimes there are baffling leaps between stanzas, as if the poet had been thinking to herself and hadn't left a complete record of her inner dialogue (the poem of Azalais de Porcairages on p. 94 is a good example). This gives the women's poems a sense of urgency that makes them more like journals than like carefully constructed works of art, although a number of them show a high level of artistic mastery.

Considering that they were probably inspired and instructed by the poems of their male contemporaries, it is interesting that the women troubadours were not the "slaves to tradition" that Alfred Jeanroy, a great French scholar, called them.

> I would imagine that our "trobairitz," slaves to tradition, incapable of analytic effort, limited themselves to exploiting the existing themes, to using the current formulas, by simply inverting the roles. We would be dealing with mere literary exercises, not, however, entirely deprived of merit.[3]

It is hard to believe that Jeanroy had even read the women troubadours or made much of an analytical effort himself. If he had, he would have noticed that the women did not exploit existing themes – unless love is a theme – and that their poems are remarkably free of formulae. Certainly they did not, as he might have wished, worship their men.

Jeanroy's judgment is an example of the kind of prejudice that has kept scholars from seeing that the women troubadours were doing something unique in medieval art: they were writing in a true first person singular at a time when almost all artistic endeavor was collective. Although the male troubadours wrote in the voice of the knight, their singular was only nominal: in fact they were expressing a vast first person plural. The difference between the women and the men can partly be accounted for by the fact that the women, as far as is known, wrote for personal rather than professional reasons. This allowed them to break out of – or ignore – the more ritualized aesthetic of the men and to use their poems as a vehicle of self-expression. Their poems are less literary and less sophisticated than the men's,

but they have an immediacy and a charm that are particularly
their own. And because their subject was themselves, the poems
provide a valuable record of the feelings of historical women
who lived and loved during the rise of *fin' amors*. They represent
the first female voices we have from a culture that has hitherto
been known only through its men. Here, truly, is the other side
of the story.

Not only do the women write in a more personal tone than
their male counterparts; the situations they depict are very
different from the courtly liaisons the men immortalized. The
most conspicuously absent figure is the humble knight:

> *Friend, if you had shown consideration,*
> *meekness, candor and humanity,*
> *I'd have loved you without hesitation,*
> *but you were mean and sly and villainous.*

Castelloza

The woman, it turns out, are not looking to be venerated;
moreover, according to the poems, there is no one around with
the slightest intention of adoring them. The men in the poems
have disappeared:

> *Handsome friend, as a lover true*
> *I loved you, for you pleased me,*
> *but now I see I was a fool,*
> *for I've barely seen you since.*

Castelloza

Some have gotten "distracted":

> *Friend, I know well enough how skilled*
> *you are in amorous affairs,*
> *and I find you rather changed*
> *from the chivalrous knight you used*
> *to be. I might as well be clear,*
> *for your mind seems quite distracted:*
> *do you still find me attractive?*

Anonymous I

LEFT: *Castelloza, from a 13th-century manuscript.*
Bibliothèque Nationale, *Ms. FR. 12473, fol. 110V.*

OPPOSITE: *Les Baux-de-Provence (Bouches-du-Rhône), home of Tibors.*
Atelier Jean-Michel Durey.

or out-and-out betrayed the women:

> *With him my mercy and fine manners are in vain,*
> *my beauty, virtue and intelligence.*
> *For I've been tricked and cheated*
> *as if I were completely loathesome.*

Countess of Dia

The men described by the women have little in common with the worshipful figures familiar from poems like the one by Guilhem de Poitou, quoted on page 38.

The women troubadours, unlike *midons*, have to argue or cajole – or grub – for every bit of attention they can get. It is through their effort to recapture or retain their men's affection that their personalities and literary skill emerge.

Some of them refer explicitly to physical love or speak of love in strongly sensual terms:

> *If only I could lie beside you for an hour*
> *and embrace you lovingly . . .*

Countess of Dia

> *Sweet handsome friend, I can tell you truly*
> *that I've never been without desire*
> *since it pleased you that I have you as my courtly lover . . .*

Tibors

Some of them explicity do *not* want sexual involvement:

We'll soon come to the test,
for I'll put myself in your hands;
you swore me your fidelity,
now don't ask me to transgress.

Azalais de Porcairages

For Clara d'Anduza, Castelloza and the woman of the third anonymous poem, love (whether physical or not we cannot tell) was the central force of their lives:

. . . for you whom I love more than anything
they've banished from my side,
and since I have no hope of seeing you again,
I die of grief, of anger, and resentment . . .

Clara d'Anduza

Castelloza is almost modern in her pursuit of a passionate attachment in which the self is risked:

I've placed my heart and soul
in jeopardy . . .

Some of the women, on the other hand, seek a rather cool relationship, in which the principal objective seems to be the exercise of arbitrary power:

Lady Iseut, if he showed some contrition
he might be able to erase
the effects of his disgrace
and I might grant him some remission . . .

Almucs de Castelnau

What do all these varied attitudes have in common? However they define *amors*, the women seek two things in their relationships: to be acknowledged for who they are, as women and as individuals, and a determining voice in how the relationship is conducted. In the *tensons* of Guillelma de Rosers, Domna H. and Maria de Ventadorn, three very different views are put forth by the women, but in all three poems the women argue for a *real,* as opposed to a *symbolic* acknowledgement of their importance. The men's arguments in all three cases are abstract; they are concerned with issues that transcend the women. The women do not want to be transcended.

Guillelma argues that if a knight has to choose between serving his lady and doing a good deed for others, he should serve his lady first. In this she strongly disagrees with her co-poet, Lanfrancs Cigala, who seems to say that by performing worthy deeds the knight is honoring his lady. This apparently trivial dialogue is actually quite significant. It opposes the male troubadour view, in which love takes on symbolic meaning and creates a moral universe, and the female, which seeks love for love's sake. The poem is also a wonderful example of the wit that often surfaced in the Provençal *tensons*.

For Domna H., courtliness is a silly game of *politesse*. In her *tenson* with a man named only as Rosin (a *senhal*), she poses the kind of question that the troubadours loved to discuss. "A lady I know," she says, "has two lovers. And she wants each of them to swear and pledge, before she'll let him near, that he's not planning to do more than hug or kiss her." One immediately grabs her (or so the poem seems to say); the other is meek and obedient. This is a bait for Rosin, who is invited to distinguish which of them deserves the lady's love. Domna H. herself is undoubtedly the lady, and Rosin is a potential lover. Her poem is a way of testing him. He fails for, like a well-schooled troubadour, he sides with the meek one. Domna H. wants unsublimated love:

> *Rosin, fear shouldn't keep*
> *a courtly lover from*
> *experiencing joy . . .*

Maria's point in her *tenson* with Gui d'Ussel puts her at odds with his advanced view of love as a relationship of equals. She has no interest in equality; she wants *superiority*:

> *. . . the lover ought to do her bidding*
> *as toward a friend and lady equally,*
> *and she should honor him the way*
> *she would a friend, but never as a lord.*

Her reluctance to be "equalized" is understandable. Equality was fine for Gui, who had everything to gain by it; for him it was a step up. For a woman of high rank, equality appeared as a step

Gui d'Ussel, from a 13th-century manuscript.
Bibliothèque Nationale, *Ms. FR. 12473, fol. 73R.*

down, and Maria clearly wasn't ready to give up the recognition
that her rank accorded her. A similar attitude is expressed in the
second anonymous poem:

> *I granted him my love on the condition*
> *he'd be mine to give away or sell,*
> *and that he'd always be at my command;*
> *but he's wronged me so gravely*
> *that he barely knows where he should hide;*
> *no, I haven't erred if I've deprived him of my love,*
> *and I won't ever lower myself for his sake.*

This woman clearly enjoys the exercise of power; she is one of
the poets who adhere most closely to the "rules" of courtly
love.

FOUR OTHER POEMS deserve particular attention. Garsenda, in
her beautifully constructed *tenson* with an unnamed man, comes
closest to speaking for the lady who desperately seeks affection
but whose social status calls for utter discretion. Her veiled
poem is like a smuggled message:

Still, in the long run it's you who stands to lose
if you're not brave enough to state your case,
and you'll do both of us great harm if you refuse.
For a lady doesn't dare uncover
her true will, lest those around her think her base.

Garsenda was in fact the highest ranking of the women troubadours. From what is known of her life it is extraordinary that she
was able to write even so cautious a poem as this. Unfortunately,
nothing is known about the circumstances of its composition.

Lombarda's testy reply to Bernard Arnaut's advances is
written in a highly witty style and is the only example of *trobar
clus*, or closed, intentionally obscure poetry, in the poems of the
women troubadours.

The *chanson* by Bieiris de Romans to a woman named Maria
(not the Virgin Mary) is the only poem by a woman troubadour
which is not concerned with heterosexual love. There is some
question about whether it was really written by a woman (see
p. 176); if it was, it is probably unique in the literature of the
Middle Ages.

The poem by three women on p. 144 is extremely curious. Much
of its meaning is unclear. It is the only poem not reflecting a
court setting, and the number of Italianisms in the language
leave its origin in doubt. Its overall message is mystical, but it
also gives a humorous and graphic view of pregnancy and
marriage and hints at the appeal of convent life for many women
of the Middle Ages.

The preceding comments open the door to twenty-three poems which have spent eight centuries in near oblivion. Much more remains to be said. Now that the women troubadours have an audience, it is hoped that other voices will soon do them fuller justice.

And now the poems, and the *trobairitz*.

A WORD ON THE TRANSLATIONS

Translation is not an art for the soft-hearted: for every nuance translated, ten are left behind. The translator's first task is to learn how to choose. Most works suggest their own priorities to the listening ear; to these the translator brings his or her own leanings.

Since the orientation of this book is more historical than literary, my role as translator has been, in the most literal sense of the word, to serve as a bringer-across, a ferrier of meaning – and to bring the Provençal across to English as intact as possible. I have therefore avoided (perhaps to the detriment of some of the translations) the notion of recreating each poem, of making poetry in English, which is widely held to be the translator's responsibility and art. I have tried, instead, to make the translations clear and readable and have adhered as closely as I could to the originals. This should enable interested readers to consult the facing texts in Provençal without confusion as to what is translated by what.

Several words remain untranslated. I have kept *lauzengier* (spy, gossip, enemy), *gelos* (jealous one) and *joglar* (singer, minstrel, messenger) mainly for their music, but also because they have no single-word equivalents in English. Words referring to poetic forms, such as *chanson*, *tenson* and *tornada*, also appear in Provençal. *En* and *Na* are the Provençal equivalents of lord and lady, respectively.

Since the Provençal poetic line had no fixed stress system I did not seek out an English meter capable of "giving the feeling" of the originals. I have, however, tried to keep the syllable count of the originals. In addition, wherever possible I have encouraged rhyme, assonance and any inner echoes that might enhance the sound-structure of each poem.

PRONUNCIATION GUIDE

SINCE THERE ARE, alas, no recordings of the troubadours, any attempt to render the exact pronunciation of their songs can only be approximate. For the English-speaking reader, the best and quickest way to an acceptable pronunciation is to think of French and Spanish at the same time, in the same breath. Somewhere in between the two Old Provençal will find its voice.

For readers who may want to read the poems aloud, the following should serve as a rough guide:

Vowels

Generally open, as in modern Spanish. *A* as in qu*a*lity, *e* intermediate between g*a*te and g*e*t, *i* as in th*e*se, *o* as in pr*o*vide, *u* as in tr*u*th: *Alamanda*, *Bieiris*, *Isabella*, *Lombarda*, *Almucs*.

In the twelfth century, an unstressed *o* preceding a stressed syllable tended toward *u*; according to Prof. Frederick Goldin, *movér* (to move) should be pronounced *muvér*. In the thirteenth century this "u-pressure" on *o* changed most stressed *o*'s to *u*'s. Thus, *Tolosa* would have been pronounced like modern French Toulouse, with an added final *a* (cf. *Castelloza*). Similarly, words ending in *or* – *amor*, *flor*, *dolor* – would rhyme with modern

French *amour*. This rule did not apply to words that ended in a double consonant (*mort, cors,* etc.).

Consonants

Follow English, with more emphatic articulation of *b, d, p* and *t*. *Ch* as in English *church*. *R* rolled as in modern Spanish or Italian. Final *g* should be pronounced *ch*: *cug* (I believe), *meg* (half). Final *z* sounds like *ts*: *genz* (people).

Two letter combinations are frequent. *Lh* sounds like the double *l* in Spanish *llanto* or the *gl* in Italian *figlia*. This sound is also indicated by *ll, il, ill, li* and *lli,* but in these variations the *i* serves only to palatalize the *l* and should not be pronounced: *uelhs* (eyes) is also written *hoills*; they sound the same and roughly rhyme with English *ways*. *Nh* should be pronounced like Spanish *ñ* in *señora*. This sound is sometimes rendered by *ng*, particularly at the end of a word.

Thirteenth and fourteenth-century scribes were masters of improvisation in orthography. There were no established rules, and it is common to find different spellings of one word within a single poem.

A vague line separates "old" and "modern" Provençal, a language spoken and/or understood by some fifteen million people in the south of France. Modern Provençal, now more generally referred to as Occitan, has been heavily influenced by French, in addition to having undergone the shifts inevitable in any language over a period of 800 years. It is still unclear to what extent it should be taken as a guideline to the pronunciation of the language spoken in the Middle Ages.

Tibors
born c.1130

Bels dous amics, ben vos posc en ver dir
que anc non fo qu'ieu estes ses desir
pos vos conven que.us tenc per fin aman;
ni anc no fo qu'ieu non agues talan,
bels dous amics, qu'ieu soven no.us vezes;
ni anc no fo sazons que m'en pentis,
ni anc no fo, se vos n'anes iratz,
qu'ieu agues joi tro que fosetz tornatz;
ni. . . .

TIBORS *is probably the earliest of the women troubadours.*
She was the sister of the troubadour Raimbaut d'Orange and the
wife of Bertrand de Baux, who was an important patron of
troubadours and lord of one of the most powerful families of
Provence. This fragment is the only poem of hers to survive.

Sweet handsome friend, I can tell you truly
that I've never been without desire
since it pleased you that I have you as my courtly lover;
nor did a time ever arrive, sweet handsome friend,
when I didn't want to see you often;
nor did I ever feel regret,
nor did it ever come to pass, if you went off angry,
that I felt joy until you had come back;
nor . . . .

Countess of Dia
born c.1140

I

Ab joi et ab joven m'apais,
e jois e jovens m'apaia,
que mos amics es lo plus gais,
per qu'ieu sui coindet' e guaia;
e pois ieu li sui veraia,
bei.s taing qu'el me sia verais:
qu'anc de lui amar non m'estrais,
ni ai cor que m'en estraia.

Mout mi plai, quar sai que val mais
cel qu'ieu plus desir que m'aia,
e cel que primiers lo m'atrais
Dieu prec que gran joi l'atraia;
e qui que mal l'en retraia,
no.l creza, fors cels qui retrais
c'om cuoill maintas vetz los balais
ab qu'el mezeis se balaia

Dompna que en bon pretz s'enten
deu ben pausar s'entendenssa
en un pro cavallier valen
pois qu'ill conois sa valenssa,
que l'aus amar a presenssa;
que dompna, pois am'a presen,
ja pois li pro ni li valen
no.n dirant mas avinenssa.

THE COUNTESS OF DIA *was probably from Die, northeast of Montélimar. She was descended from seigneurial families of the Viennois and Burgundy and was married to a lord of Die. Four of her poems have survived.*

I

I thrive on youth and joy,
and youth and joy keep me alive,
for my friend's the very gayest,
which makes me gay and playful;
and since I'm true,
he should be faithful:
my love for him has never strayed,
nor is my heart the straying kind.

I'm very happy, for the man
whose love I seek's so fine.
May God with joy richly repay
the man who helped us meet.
If anyone should disagree,
pay him no heed; listen only
to the one who knows one often picks the blooms
from which one's own broom's made.*

The lady who knows about valor
should place her affection
in a courteous and worthy knight
as soon as she has seen his worth,
and she should dare to love him face to face;
for courteous and worthy men
can only speak with great esteem
of a lady who loves openly.

* Probably a proverb. Literally, "For one often picks the brooms with which one sweeps oneself;" i.e., "One is often responsible for one's own undoing."

Qu'ieu n'ai chausit un pro e gen,
per cui pretz meillur' e genssa,
larc et adreig e conoissen,
on es sens e conoissenssa.
Prec li que m'aia crezenssa,
ni om no.l puosca far crezen
qu'ieu fassa vas lui faillimen,
sol non trob en lui faillensa.

Amics, la vostra valenssa
sabon li pro e li valen,
per qu'ieu vos quier de mantenen,
si.us plai, vostra mantenenssa.

II

A chantar m'er de so qu'ieu non volria,
tant me rancur de lui cui sui amia,
car l'am mais que nuilla ren que sia;
vas lui no.m val merces ni cortesia,
ni ma beltatz ni mos pretz ni mos sens,
c'atressi.m sui enganad' e trahia
com degr' esser, s'ieu fos desavinens.

D'aisso.m conort car anc non fi faillenssa,
amics, vas vos per nuilla captenenssa,
anz vos am mais non fetz Seguis Valenssa;
e platz me mout quez eu d'amar vos venssa,
lo mieus amics, car etz lo plus valens;
mi faitz orguoill en ditz et en parvenssa,
e si etz francs vas totas autras gens.

I've picked a fine and noble man,
in whom merit shines and ripens –
generous, upright and wise,
with intelligence and common sense.
I pray him to believe my words
and not let anyone persuade him
that I ever would betray him,
except I found myself betrayed.

Floris,* your worth
is known to all good men;
therefore I make this request:
please, grant me your protection.

II

Of things I'd rather keep in silence I must sing:
so bitter do I feel toward him
whom I love more than anything.
With him my mercy and fine manners are in vain,
my beauty, virtue and intelligence.
For I've been tricked and cheated
as if I were completely loathesome.

There's one thing, though, that brings me recompense:
I've never wronged you under any circumstance,
and I love you more than Seguin loved Valensa.†
At least in love I have my victory,
since I surpass the worthiest of men.
With me you always act so cold,
but with everyone else you're so charming.

---

* Probably a *senhal*; Floris was the hero of a popular romance, now lost (see Countess of Dia, poem III).
† Hero and heroine, respectively, of a lost romance.

Be.m meravill com vostre cors s'orguoilla,
amics, vas me, per qu'ai razon qu'ieu.m duoilla;
non es ges dreitz c'autr' amors vos mi tuoilla
per nuilla ren que.us diga ni acuoilla;
e membre vos cals fo.l comenssamens
de nostr' amor! ja Dompnedieus non vuoilla
qu'en ma colpa sia.l departimens.

Proesa grans qu'el vostre cors s'aizina
e lo rics pretz qu'avetz m'en ataïna,
c'una non sai, loindana ni vezina,
si vol amar, vas vos non si' aclina;
mas vos, amics, etz ben tant conoissens
que ben devetz conoisser la plus fina:
e membre vos de nostres partimens.

Valer mi deu mos pretz e mos paratges,
e ma beltatz e plus mos fis coratges,
per qu'ieu vos mand lai on es vostr' estatges
esta chansson que me sia messatges;
ieu vuoill saber, lo mieus bels amics gens,
per que vos m'etz tant fers ni tant salvatges;
non sai si s'es orguoills o mal talens.

Mas aitan plus vuoill li digas, messatges,
qu'en trop d'orguoill ant gran dan maintas gens.

I have good reason to lament
when I feel your heart turn adamant
toward me, friend: it's not right another love
take you away from me, no matter what she says.
Remember how it was with us in the beginning
of our love! May God not bring to pass
that I should be the one to bring it to an end.

The great renown that in your heart resides
and your great worth disquiet me,
for there's no woman near or far
who wouldn't fall for you if love were on her mind.
But you, my friend, should have the acumen
to tell which one stands out above the rest.
And don't forget the stanzas we exchanged.

My worth and noble birth should have some weight,
my beauty and especially my noble thoughts;
so I send you, there on your estate,
this song as messenger and delegate.
I want to know, my handsome noble friend,
why I deserve so savage and so cruel a fate.
I can't tell whether it's pride or malice you intend.

But above all, messenger, make him comprehend
that too much pride has undone many men.

III

Estat ai en greu cossirier
per un cavallier qu'ai agut,
e vuoil sia totz temps saubut
cum ieu l'ai amat a sobrier;
ara vei qu'ieu sui trahida
car ieu non li donei m'amor,
don ai estat en gran error
en lieig e quand sui vestida.

Ben volria mon cavallier
tener un ser en mos bratz nut,
qu'el s'en tengra per ereubut
sol qu'a lui fezes cosseillier;
car plus m'en sui abellida
no fetz Floris de Blanchaflor:
ieu l'autrei mon cor e m'amor,
mon sen, mos huoills e ma vida.

Bels amics avinens e bos,
cora.us tenrai en mon poder?
e que jagues ab vos un ser
e qu'ie.us des un bais amoros;
sapchatz, gran talan n'auria
qu'ie.us tengues en luoc del marit,
ab so que m'aguessetz plevit
de far tot so qu'ieu volria.

III

I've lately been in great distress
over a knight who once was mine,
and I want it known for all eternity
how I loved him to excess.
Now I see I've been betrayed
because I wouldn't sleep with him;*
night and day† my mind won't rest
to think of the mistake I made.

How I wish just once I could caress
that chevalier with my bare arms,
for he would be in ecstasy
if I'd just let him lean his head against my breast.
I'm sure I'm happier with him
than Blancaflor with Floris.††
My heart and love I offer him,
my mind, my eyes, my life.

Handsome friend, charming and kind,
when shall I have you in my power?
If only I could lie beside you for an hour
and embrace you lovingly –
know this, that I'd give almost anything
to have you in my husband's place,
but only under the condition
that you swear to do my bidding.

---

* Some scholars see in this line a classic reference to the *épreuve*, or test of chastity,
which required the lovers to sleep together naked with a sword between them.
† Literally, "in bed and when I'm dressed."
†† Heroine and hero, respectively, of a lost popular romance.

IV

Fin ioi me don' alegranssa,
per qu'eu chan plus gaiamen,
e no m'o teing a pensanssa,
ni a negun penssamen,
car sai que son a mon dan
fals lausengier e truan,
e lor mals diz non m'esglaia:
anz en son dos tanz plus gaia.

En mi non an ges fianssa
li lauzengier mal dizen,
c'om non pot aver honranssa
qu'a ab els acordamen;
qu'ist son d'altrestal semblan
com la niuols que s'espan
qe.l solels en pert sa raia,
per qu'eu non am gent savaia.

E vos, gelos mal parlan,
no.s cuges que m'an tarzan,
que iois e iovenz no.m plaia,
per tal que dols vos deschaia.

IV

Fine joy brings me great happiness,*
which makes me sing more gaily,
and it doesn't bother me a bit
or weigh my spirit down
that those sneaky *lauzengiers*†
are out to do me harm;
their evil talk doesn't dismay me,
it just makes me twice as gay.

Those nasty-worded *lauzengiers*
won't get an ounce of trust from me,
for no one will find honor
who has anything to do with them.
They are like the cloud that grows
and billows out until
the sun loses its rays:
I have no use for such as them.

And you, gossiping *gelos*,††
don't think I'm going to hang around,
or that joy and youth§ don't please me:
beware, or grief will bring you low.

---

* "Fine" in the sense of "courtly," as in *fin' amors,* courtly love.
† Omnipresent characters in troubadour love poetry. *Lauzengiers* were spies in the employ of the jealous husband; they not only eavesdropped on the lovers but did everything possible to thwart their secret meetings. The figure of the *lauzengier* probably corresponds to the very real difficulty of finding privacy in the courtly setting.
†† *Gelos* is almost always used in Provençal to designate the jealous husband, an indispensable third party to any properly conducted courtly liaison.
§ *Iois e iovenz* may here be taken as a single term designating courtly love. "Joy" and "youth" were the essential qualities of any courtly lover, male or female.

Almucs de Castelnau and Iseut de Capio
born c.1140

Dompna n'Almucs, si.us plages
be.us volgra pregar d'aitan
que l'ira e.l mal talan
vos fezes tenir merces
de lui que sospir' e plaing,
e muor languent e.s complaing
e quier perdon humilmen;
be.us fatz per lui sagramen,
si tot li voletz fenir,
qu'el si gart meilz de faillir.

Dompna n'Iseus, s'ieu saubes
qu'el se pentis de l'engan
qu'el a fait vas mi tan gran,
ben fora dreich que n'agues
merces; mas a mi no.s taing,
pos que del tort no s'afraing
ni.s pentis del faillimen,
que n'aja mais chauzimen;
mas si vos faitz lui pentir,
leu podretz mi convertir.

ALMUCS DE CASTELNAU AND ISEUT DE CAPIO *were from two neighboring towns of Provence, about thirty miles due east of Avignon in the valley of the Lubéron. Almucs was probably a patron of troubadours, as was her son, Raimbaut d'Agoult.*

Lady Almucs, with your permission
let me request that in place
of anger and bad grace
you show a kinder disposition
toward him who slowly dying lies
lamenting amidst moans and sighs
and humbly begs reprieve;
but if you want him dead let him receive
the sacraments, to guarantee
that he'll refrain from doing further injury.

Lady Iseut, if he showed some contrition
he might be able to erase
the effects of his disgrace
and I might grant him some remission;
but I think I'd be unwise,
since by his silence he denies
the wrong he's done, to in any way relieve
a man who was so eager to deceive.
Still, if you can get him to repent his perfidy
you'll have no trouble in converting me.

Azalais de Porcairages
born c.1140

Ar em al freg temps vengut
quel gels el neus e la faingna
e.l aucellet estan mut,
c'us de chantar non s'afraingna;
e son sec li ram pels plais –
que flors ni foilla noi nais,
ni rossignols noi crida,
que l'am e mai me reissida.

Tant ai lo cors deseubut,
pe qu'ieu soi a totz estraingna,
e sai que l'om a perdut
molt plus tost que non gasaingna;
e s'ieu faill ab motz verais,
d'Aurenga me moc l'esglais,
per qu'ieu m'estauc esbaïda
e 'n pert solatz en partida.

Dompna met mot mal s'amor
que ab ric ome plaideia,
ab plus aut de vavassor;
e s'il o fai, il folleia,
car so diz om en Veillai
que ges per ricor non vai,
e dompna que n'es chauzida
en tenc per envilanida.

AZALAIS DE PORCAIRAGES *was from the modern town of Portiragnes, just outside Béziers. Nothing definite is known about her life, but she appears to have moved in courtly society.*

Now we are come to the cold time
when the ice and the snow and the mud
and the birds' beaks are mute
(for not one inclines to sing);
and the hedge-branches are dry –
no leaf nor bud sprouts up,
nor cries the nightingale
whose song awakens me in May.*

My heart is so disordered
that I'm rude to everyone;
I know it's easier to lose
than gain; still, though I be blamed
I'll tell the truth:
my pain comes from Orange.†
That's why I stand gaping,
for I've lost the joy of solace.

A lady's love is badly placed
who argues with a wealthy man,
one above the rank of vassal:
she who does it is a fool.
For the people of Vélay††
say love and money do not mix,
and the woman money chooses
they say has lost her honor.

---

* This line recalls the May songs of the popular tradition.
† Perhaps a reference to Raimbaut d'Orange.
†† Corresponds to the southern part of the Auvergne.

Amic ai de gran valor
que sobre toz seignoreia,
e non a cor trichador
vas me, que s'amor m'autreia.
Ieu dic que m'amors l'eschai,
e cel que dis que non fai,
Dieus li don mal' escarida,
qu'ieu m'en teing fort per guerida.

Bels amics, de bon talan
son ab vos toz jornz en gatge,
cortez' e de bel semblan,
sol no.m demandes outratge;
tost en venrem a l'assai,
qu'en vostra merce.m metrai:
vos m'avetz la fe plevida,
que no.m demandes faillida.

A Dieu coman Bel Esgar
e plus la ciutat d'Aurenza,
e Glorïet' e.l Caslar,
e lo seignor de Proenza
e tot can vol mon ben lai,
e l'arc on son fag l'assai.
Celui perdiei c'a ma vida,
e 'n serai toz jorns marrida.

Joglar, que avetz cor gai,
ves Narbona portatz lai
ma chanson ab la fenida
lei cui jois e jovens guida.

I have a friend of great repute
who towers above all other men,
and his heart toward me is not untrue, for he offers me his love.
And I tell you I reciprocate,
and whoever says I don't,
God curse his luck –
as for myself, I know I'm safe.

Handsome friend, I'd gladly stay
forever in your service –
such noble mien and such fine looks –
so long as you don't ask too much;
we'll soon come to the test,
for I'll put myself in your hands:
you swore me your fidelity,
now don't ask me to transgress.

To God I commend Bel Esgar
and the city of Orange,
and Gloriet' and the Caslar,
and the lord of all Provence,
and all those there who wish me well,
and the arch where the attacks are shown.*
I've lost the man who owns my life,
and I shall never be consoled.

Joglar, you of merry heart,
carry my song down to Narbonne,
with its *tornada* made for her†
whose guides are youth and joy.

---

* The Roman arch of Orange was one of the outstanding monuments of medieval
Provence (see illustration, p. 42). The other references in the stanza are to now
unknown landmarks, presumably also in the area of Orange.
† Probably the Viscountess Ermengarda of Narbonne, a major political and cultural
figure over a period of fifty years.

Maria de Ventadorn
born c.1165

Gui d'Ussel, be.m pesa de vos,
car vos etz laissatz de chantar,
e car vos i volgra tornar,
per que sabetz d'aitals razos,
vuoill que.m digatz, si deu far egalmen
dompna per drut, can lo quier francamen,
cum el per lieis tot cant taing ad amor
segon los dreitz que tenon l'amador.

Dompna na Maria, tenssos
e tot chant cuiava laissar,
mas aoras non puosc estar
qu'ieu non chant als vostres somos;
e respon vos de la dompna breumen
que per son drut deu far comunalmen
cum el per lieis, ses garda de ricor:
qu'en dos amics non deu aver maior.

MARIA DE VENTADORN *was from the Limousin. She was the daughter of a viscount and, along with her two sisters, one of the "Tres de Torena" sung by Bertran de Born. She was married to Ebles V de Ventadorn, lord of a neighboring viscounty and a well-known patron of troubadours.*

Maria's tenson *with Gui d'Ussel is one of the few poems by a woman troubadour which have a* razo, *or* joglar's *paraphrase of the song he was about to sing. The* razos *are pure invention. They are often quite charming, and this one, the text of which is printed on p. 168, gives a good idea of the kind of tale the courtly audience enjoyed.*

Gui d'Ussel, because of you I'm quite distraught,
for you've given up your song,
and since I wish you'd take it up again,
and since you know about such things,
I'll ask you this: when a lady
freely loves a man, should she do
as much for him as he for her,
according to the rules of courtly love?

Lady Maria, *tensons*
and all manner of song
I thought I'd given up,
but when you summon, how can I refuse to sing?
My reply is that the lady
ought to do exactly for her lover
as he does for her, without regard to rank;
for between two friends neither one should rule.

Gui, tot so don es cobeitos
deu drutz ab merce demandar,
e dompna deu l'o autreiar,
mas ben deu esgardar sazos;
e.l drutz deu far precs e comandamen
cum per amig' e per dompn' eissamen,
e dompna deu a son drut far honor
cum ad amic, mas non cum a seignor.

Dompna, sai dizon de mest nos
que, pois que dompna vol amar,
egalmen deu son drut onrar,
pois egalmen son amoros;
e s'esdeven que l'am plus finamen,
e.l faich e.l dich en deu far aparen,
e si ell' a fals cor ni trichador,
ab bel semblan deu cobrir sa follor.

Gui d'Uissel, ges d'aitals razos
non son li drut al comenssar,
anz ditz chascus, can vol preiar,
mans jointas e de genolhos:
"Dompna, voillatz que.us serva francamen
cum lo vostr' om," et ell' enaissi.l pren;
ieu lo jutge per dreich a trahitor,
si.s rend pariers ei.s det per servidor.

Dompna, so es plaich vergoignos,
ad ops de dompna razonar,
que cellui non teigna per par
ab cui a faich un cor de dos.
O vos diretz, e no.us estara gen,
que.l drutz la deu amar plus leialmen,
o vos diretz qu'il son par entre lor,
pois ren no.lh deu drutz mas quant per amor.

Gui, the lover humbly ought to ask
for everything his heart desires,
and the lady should comply with his request
within the bounds of common sense;
and the lover ought to do her bidding
as toward a friend and lady equally,
and she should honor him the way
she would a friend, but never as a lord.

Lady, here the people say
that when a lady wants to love
she owes her lover equal honor
since they're equally in love.
And if it happens that she loves him more,
her words and deeds should make it show;
but if she's fickle or untrue
she ought to hide it with a pretty face.

Gui d'Ussel, suitors when they're new
are not at all like that,
for when they seek a lady's grace
they get down on their knees, hands joined, and say:
"Grant that I may freely serve you, lady,
as your man," and she receives them;
thus to me it's nothing short of treason
if a man says he's her equal *and* her servant.

Lady, it's embarrassing
to argue that a lady should
be higher than the man with whom
she's made one heart of two.
Either you'll say (and this won't flatter you)
that the man should love the lady more,
or else you'll say that they're the same,
because the lover doesn't owe her anything that doesn't bear
love's name.*

---

* i.e., whatever the lady's rank, it does not entitle her to act superior; love is the great
leveler.

Alamanda
fl. second half of 12th century

S'ie.us quier conseill, bell' ami' Alamanda,
no.l me vedetz, qu'om cochatz lo.us demanda,
que so m'a dich vostra dompna truanda
que loing sui fors issitz de sa comanda,
que so que.m det m'estrai er e.m desmanda;
que.m cosseillatz?
qu'a pauc lo cors totz d'ira no.m abranda,
tan fort en sui iratz.

Per Dieu, Giraut, jes aissi tot a randa
volers d'amics noi.s fai ni noi.s garanda,
que, si l'uns faill, l'autre coven que blanda,
que lor destrics noi.s cresca ni s'espanda;
e s'ela.us ditz d'aut puoig que sia landa,
vos la 'n crezatz,
e plassa vos lo bes e.l mals qu'il manda,
qu'aissi seretz amatz.

Non puosc mudar que contr' orguoill non gronda,
ja siatz vos donzella bell' e blonda;
pauc d'ira.us notz e paucs jois vos aonda,
mas jes non etz primieira ni segonda.
Ieu que.m tem fort d'est ira que.m confonda –
vos me lauzatz,
si.m sent perir, que.m tenga plus vas l'onda:
mal cre que.m capdellatz.

ALAMANDA *may have been a Gascon. Our only knowledge of her
comes from the* vida *of Guiraut de Bornelh, one of the major
troubadours of the classical period, with whom she exchanged
her* tenson.

If I seek your advice, pretty friend Alamanda,
don't make things hard for me, for I'm a banished man.
For that's what your deceitful mistress told me,
that now I've been expelled from her command:
and what she gave me she retracts now and reclaims.
What should I do?
I'm so angry that my body's
all but bursting into flame.

In God's name, Guiraut, a lover's wishes
count for nothing here, for if one partner fails
the other should keep up appearances
so that their trouble doesn't spread or grow.
If she tells you that a high peak is a plain,
believe her,
and accept the good *and* bad she sends:
thus shall you be loved.

I can't keep from speaking out against her pride,
even if you're young and beautiful and blond.
The slightest pain hurts me, the smallest joy overwhelms,
and still I'm not in first or second place.*
I'm worried that this anger will destroy me:
you praise me,
but I can tell – I'm closer to the waves†
and I think you're leading me astray.

---

* In other words. "I'm sensitive the way a courtly lover is supposed to be, and still it
gets me nowhere with her." The Provençal uses "you" (*vos*) in the sense of "one".
† *Onda* – wave – is probably a misreading of *ongla*, fingernail; this would be less
interesting but a much more common metaphor in Provençal.

Si m'enqueretz d'aital razon prionda,
per Dieu, Giraut, non sai, com vos responda;
vos m'apellatz de leu cor jauzionda –
mais vuoill pelar mon prat qu'autre.l mi tonda;
que s'ie.us era del plaich far desironda,
vos escercatz;
com son bel cors vos esdui' e.us resconda,
ben par com n'etz cochatz.

Donzell', oimais non siatz tant parlieira,
qu'il m'a mentit mais de cinc vetz primieira;
cujatz vos doncs qu'ieu totz temps lo sofieira?
Semblaria qu'o fezes per nescieira.
D'autr' amistat ai talan qu'ie.us enquieira,
si no.us calatz;
meillor cosseil dava na Barengieira
que vos non m'en donatz.

Lora vei ieu, Giraut, qu'ela.us o mieira,
car l'apelletz camjairitz ni leugieira;
pero cujatz que del plaich vos enquieira?
Ieu non cuig jes qu'il sia tant mainieira:
ans er oimais sa proeza derreira,
que que.us digatz,
si.s destrenh tant que contra vos sofieira
trega ni fi ni patz.

Bella, per Dieu, non perga vostr' ajuda;
ja sabetz vos com mi fo covenguda;
s'ieu ai faillit per l'ira qu'ai aguda,
no.m tenga dan; s'anc sentitz com leu muda
cors d'amador, bella, e s'anc fotz druda,
del plaich pensatz!
qu'ieu sui be mortz, s'enaissi l'ai perduda;
mas no.lh o descobratz!

If you come to me with questions so profound,
my God, Guiraut, I don't know what to say.
You call to me with a joyful, easy heart,
but I want to mow my field before someone else tries;*
if I wanted to arrange a peace
I would have looked for you,
but since she keeps her lovely body hidden so,
I think you're right that you've been ditched.

Now don't start yakking, young girl,
for she lied to me first, more than five times.
Do you think I can put up with this much more?
I'd be taken for an ignoramus.
I have a mind to ask about another friendship
if you don't shut up;
I got much better counsel from Na Berengeira†
than I ever got from you.

Now I see, Guiraut, that she's capable of everything,
since you call her fickle and unfaithful;
still, do you think she wants to patch things up?
I doubt she's that tame yet:
from now on she'll keep courtesy in last place,
no matter what you say.
She's so angry with you that she'll suffer
neither peace nor oath nor treaty.

Beauty, for God's sake, don't let me lose your aid –
you already know how it was granted me.
If I've done wrong in being so irate,
don't hold it against me; and if you've ever felt how fast
a lover's heart can change, or if you've ever loved,
think of some way;
for I'm as good as dead if I have lost her –
but don't tell her that.

* The exact meaning of this line is obscure.
† Unknown noblewoman. Perhaps the wife of one of the many Raimon Berengars of Provence.

Seign' en Giraut, ja n'agr' ieu fin volguda,
mas ella ditz qu'a dreich s'es irascuda,
qu'autra 'n prejetz com fols tot a saubuda
que non la val ni vestida ni nuda;
noi fara doncs, si no.us gic, que vencuda,
s'autra 'n prejatz?
Be.us en valrai et ai la.us manteguda,
si mais no.us i mesclatz.

Bella, per Dieu, si de lai n'etz crezuda,
per me l'o affiatz!

Ben o farai, mas, quan vos er renduda
s'amors, non la.us toillatz.

Seigneur Guiraut, I didn't want your love to end,
but she says she has a right to be enraged,
because you're courting someone else in front of everyone
who next to her's worth nothing, clothed or nude.
If she didn't jilt you she'd be acting weak,
since you're courting someone else.
But I'll speak well of you to her – I always have –
if you promise not to keep on doing that.

Beauty, for God's sake, if she has your trust,
promise her for me.

I'll gladly do so, but when she's given you her love again,
don't take yours back.

Garsenda
born c.1170

Vos que.m semblatz dels corals amadors,
ja non volgra que fossetz tan doptanz;
e platz me molt quar vos destreing m'amors,
qu'atressi sui eu per vos malananz.
Ez avetz dan en vostre vulpillatge
quar no.us ausatz de preiar enardir,
e faitz a vos ez a mi gran dampnatge;
que ges dompna non ausa descobrir
tot so qu'il vol per paor de faillir.

Bona dompna, vostr' onrada valors
mi fai temeros estar, tan es granz,
e no.m o tol negun' autra paors
qu'eu non vos prec; que.us volria enanz
tan gen servir que non fezes oltratge –
qu'aissi.m sai eu de preiar enardir –
e volria que.l faich fosson messatge,
e presessetz en loc de precs servir:
qu'us honratz faitz deu be valer un dir.

GARSENDA DE FORCALQUIER *belonged by birth to one of the leading families of Provence, by marriage to another. Her husband was Alphonse II, lord of Provence and brother of the King of Aragon. After his death she ruled Provence. Her partner in this* tenson *remains anonymous.*

You're so well-suited as a lover,
I wish you wouldn't be so hesitant;
but I'm glad my love makes *you* the penitent,
otherwise I'd be the one to suffer.
Still, in the long run it's you who stands to lose
if you're not brave enough to state your case,
and you'll do both of us great harm if you refuse.
For a lady doesn't dare uncover
her true will, lest those around her think her base.

Good lady, it's your rank that makes me shudder,
your high birth that thwarts my good intent –
because of that alone I'm reticent.
You know I'd rather serve you as a brother
than do anything that would abuse you
(you see, I *do* know how to state my case).
If only deeds were messengers to you,
and you accepted *them* in wooing's place:
for noble deeds, as much as words, deserve your grace.

Isabella
born c.1180

N'Elias Cairel, de l'amor
qu'ieu e vos soliam aver
voil, si.us platz, que.m digatz lo ver,
per que l'avetz cambiad' aillor;
que vostre chanz non vai si com solia,
et anc vas vos no.m sui salvatz un dia,
ni vos d'amor no.m demandetz anc tan
qu'ieu non fezes tot al vostre coman.

Ma domn' Isabella, valor
joi e pretz e sen e saber
soliatz quec jorn mantener,
e s'ieu en dizia lauzor
en mon chantar, no.l dis per drudaria,
mas per honor e pro qu'ieu n'atendia,
si com joglars fai de domna prezan;
mas chascun jorn m'etz anada cambian.

N'Elias Cairel, amador
non vi mais de vostre voler,
qui cambies domna per aver,
e s'ieu en disses desonor
ieu n'ai dig tant de be qu'om no.l creiria;
mas ben podetz doblar vostra follia:
de mi vos dic qu'ades vau meilluran,
mas endreig vos non ai cor ni talan.

Nothing concrete is known about ISABELLA. *She may have been the daughter of a nobleman from one of the Christian empires of the East. Elias Cairel, with whom she exchanged this* tenson, *was a troubadour from Périgord.*

Elias Cairel, I want to know
the truth about the love we two
once had; so tell me, please,
why you've given it to someone else.
For your song doesn't sound the way it did,
and I never held myself back from you,
nor did you once demand such love from me
but that I wasn't instantly at your command.

My lady Isabella, in those days
you showed dignity
and joy and strength and wit and wisdom,
but if I sang your praises
it wasn't out of love
but for the profit I might get from it,
just as any joglar sings a lady's fame:
but you kept changing every day.

Elias Cairel, I've never seen
a lover who would trade
his lady's love for riches,
and if I were to speak against him,
I've so often praised him no one would believe me.
Go ahead, double your insanity:
as for me, I'm much improved,
although for you I have no use.

Domna, ieu faria gran follor,
s'estes gair' en vostre poder,
e ges per tal no.m desesper,
s'anc tot non aic pro ni honor;
vos remanretz tals com la genz vos cria,
et ieu irei vezer ma bell' amia
e.l sieu gen cors grail' e ben estan,
que no.m a cor menzongier ni truan.

N'Elias Cairel, fegnedor
resemblatz segon mon parer,
com hom qui.s feing de dol aver
de so dont el non sent dolor.
Si.m creziatz, bon conseil vos daria:
que tornassetz estar en la badia,
e no.us auzei anc mais dir mon semblan,
mas pregar n'ei lo patrïarch' Ivan.

Domn' Isabel, en refreitor
non estei anc mattin ni ser,
mas vos n'auretz oimais lezer,
qu'en breu temps perdretz la color;
estier mon grat mi faitz dir vilania,
et ai mentit, qu'ieu non crei qu'el mond sia
domna tant pros ni ab beutat tant gran
com vos avetz, per qu'ieu ai agut dan.

Si.us plazia, n'Elias, ieu volria
que.m disessetz, quals es la vostr' amia,
e digatz lo.m e no i anetz doptan,
qu'ieu.us en valrai, s'ela val ni a sen tan.

Domna, vos m'enqueretz de gran follia,
que per razon s'amistat en perdria,
e per paor que lauzengier mi fan,
pero non aus descubrir mon talan.

Lady, I'd be crazy to remain
another day in your domain;
still, I don't despair
just because I don't have fame and profit;
you will stay the way the people want you,
and I'll go pay a visit to my pretty friend
whose body's graceful and well-kept,
whose heart is neither lying nor deceitful.

Elias Cairel, you're a phoney
if I ever saw one,
like a man who says he's sick
when he hasn't got the slightest pain.
If you'd listen, I'd give you good advice:
go back to your cloister,
and don't dare pronounce my name again
except in prayer to the patriarch Ivan.*

Lady Isabella, in a monks' refectory
I've never taken morn nor evening meal,
but you'll have ample opportunity
for your fresh color will soon fade.
Against my will you make me say cruel things,
and I have lied: for there's no woman
worthier than you, nor one more beautiful
in the whole world; that's why I suffer.

If you don't mind, Elias,
I'd like to know who your new lady is:
so tell me, and don't be afraid,
that I may judge her worth and her intelligence.

Lady, what you ask would be a foolish thing;
I don't want to risk her friendship,
and I'm scared the *lauzengiers* will talk:
therefore I don't dare speak my desire.

* Obscure reference; probably a patriarch of the Eastern Church.

Lombarda
born c.1190

I

Lombards volgr'eu esser per na Lombarda,
qu'Alamanda no.m plaz tan ni Giscarda,
qar ab sos oiltz plaisenz tan jen mi garda
qe par qe.m don s'amor, mas trop me tarda.

    Qar bel vezer
    e mon plaiser
    ten e bel ris en garda,
    c'om no.ls ne pod mover.

Seigner Jordan, se vos lais Alamagna
Frans' e Piteus, Normandi' e Bretagna,
be me devez laisar senes mesclagna
e Lombardi' e Livorn'e Lomagna.

    E si.m valez,
    eu per un dez
    valdre.us ab leis qu'estragna
    es de tot avol prez.

    Mirail de prez,
    c'onor avez,
    ges per vila no.s fragna
    l'amors en qe.m tenez.

LOMBARDA *appears to have been from Toulouse. She is one of the few women troubadours to write in* trobar clus, *the hermetic, "closed" style of some of the best Provençal poets. Her* tenson *with Barnat Arnaut d'Armagnac is in two sections, rather than the customary alternating stanza pattern. Part I is spoken by Bernart Arnaut, part II by Lombarda.*

I

I'd like to be a Lombard for Lombarda,
for I like her more than Alamanda or Giscarda;
I like the way her pretty eyes regard me,
as if to offer me her love – but how she makes me wait!

For beauty, laughter,
and my pleasure
she has under lock and key
where nobody can get.

Lord Jordan, if I leave you Germany,
France, Poitiers, Normandy and Brittany,
then you should leave me without argument
Lombardy, Livorno and Lomagna.

And if you're worthy
I'll increase your worth
tenfold with her who's foreign
to all evilness.

Merit's mirror,
who hath honor,
don't let that good-for-nothing
break the love that binds us.

II

No.m volgr' aver per Bernard na Bernarda
e per n'Arnaut n'Arnauda appellada,
e grans merces, seigner, car vos agrada
c'ab tals doas domnas m'aves nommada.

    Voil qe'm digaz
    cals mais vos plaz
    ses cuberta selada
    e.l mirail on miratz.

Car lo mirailz e no veser descorda
tan mon acord c'ab pauc no.l desacorda,
mas can record so qu'l meus noms recorda,
en bon acord totz mons pensars s'acorda.

    Mas del cor pes
    on l'aves mes,
    que sa maiso ni borda
    no vei, que las taises.

II

I'm glad I wasn't called Bernarda for Bernart,
and that I wasn't named Arnauda for Arnaut;
but many thanks, lord, since it gives you pleasure
to name me side by side with two such ladies.*

    I want to know
    your true opinion:
    which one you prefer, and what's
    the mirror where you stare.

For the mirror with no image so disrupts
my rhyme that it almost interrupts it;
but then when I remember what my name records,
all my thoughts unite in one accord.

    But I wonder
    where your heart is,
    for it's house and hearth
    are hid, and you won't tell.

---

* Alamanda's reply makes fun of Bernart Arnaut's precious first stanza. Occitanian
women often took their husband's name when they married; Lombarda plays on this
and makes herself into two "wives" of Bernart Arnaut – they are unreal, like "the
mirror with no image" of her third stanza. He, she seems to say, is in love with his
own image.

Castelloza
born c.1200

I

Amics, s'ie.us trobes avinen,
humil e franc e de bona merce,
be.us amera, quan era m'en sove
que.us trob vas mi mal e fellon e tric;
e fauc chanssos per tal qu'ieu fass' auzir
vostre bon pretz, don ieu non puosc sofrir
que no.us fassa lauzar a tota gen,
on plus mi faitz mal et adiramen.

Jamais no.us tenrai per valen
ni.us amarai de bon cor e de fe,
tro que veirai si ja.m valria re
si.us mostrava cor fellon ni enic;
non farai ja, car non vuoill poscatz dir
qu'ieu anc vas vos agues cor de faillir,
qu'auriatz pois qualque razonamen,
s'ieu fazia vas vos nuill faillimen.

Ieu sai ben qu'a mi estai gen
si bei.s dizon tuich que mout descove
que dompna prei a cavallier de se
ni que.l teigna totz temps tan loc prezic;
mas cel qu'o ditz non sap ges ben chausir,
qu'ieu vuoill proar enans que.m lais morir
qu'el preiar ai un gran revenimen
quan prec cellui don ai greu pessamen.

*CASTELLOZA was from the Auvergne, from the region of Le Puy.
She was probably the wife of a nobleman who fought in the
Fourth Crusade. Three of her poems have survived.*

I

Friend, if you had shown consideration,
meekness, candor and humanity,
I'd have loved you without hesitation;
but you were mean and sly and villainous.
Still, I make this song to spread your praises
wide, for I can't bare to let your name
go on unsung and unrenowned,
no matter how much worse you treat me now.

I won't consider you a decent man
nor love you fully nor with trust
until I see if it would help me more
to make my heart turn mean or treacherous.
But I don't want to give you an excuse
for saying I was ever devious with you;
something you could keep in store
in case I never did you wrong.

It greatly pleases me
when people say that it's unseemly
for a lady to approach a man she likes
and hold him deep in conversation;
but whoever says that isn't very bright,
and I want to prove before you let me die
that courting brings me great relief
when I court the man who's brought me grief.

Assatz es fols qui m'en repren
de vos amar, pois tan gen mi cove,
e cel qu'o ditz no sap cum s'es de me;
ni no.us vei ges aras si cum vos vic
quan me dissetz que non agues cossir
que calqu'ora poiri' endevenir
que n'auria enqueras jauzimen:
de sol lo dich n'ai ieu lo cor jauzen.

Tot' autr' amor teing a nïen,
e sapchatz ben que mais jois no.m soste
mas lo vostre que m'alegr' e.m reve,
on mais en sent d'afan e de destric;
e.m cuig ades alegrar e jauzir
de vos, amics, qu'ieu non puosc convertir,
ni joi non ai, ni socors non aten,
mas sol aitan quan n'aurai en dormen.

Oimais non sai que.us mi presen,
que cercat ai et ab mal et ab be
vostre dur cor, don lo mieus noi.s recre;
e no.us o man, qu'ieu mezeissa.us o dic:
que morai me, si no.m voletz jauzir
de qualque joi, e si.m laissatz morir,
faretz peccat, e serai n'en tormen,
e seretz ne blasmatz vilanamen.

Whoever blames my love for you's
a fool, for it greatly pleases me,
and whoever says that doesn't know me;
I don't see you now at all the way I did
the time you said I shouldn't worry,
since at any moment I might
rediscover reason to rejoice:
from words alone my heart is full of joy.

All other love's worth naught,
and every joy is meaningless to me
but yours, which gladdens and restores me,
in which there's not a trace of pain or of distress;
and I think I'll be glad always and rejoice
always in you, friend, for I can't convert;
nor have I any joy, nor do I find relief,
but what little solace comes to me in sleep.

I don't know why you're always on my mind,
for I've searched and searched from good to evil
your hard heart, and yet my own's unswerving.
I don't send you this; no, I tell you myself:
if you don't want me to enjoy
the slightest happiness, then I shall die;
and if you let me die, you'll be a guilty man;
I'll be in my grave, and you'll be cruelly blamed.

II

Ja de chantar non degr' aver talan,
quar on mais chan
e pietz me vai d'amor,
que plaing e plor
fan en mi lor estatge;
car en mala merce
ai mes mon cor e me,
e s'en breu no.m rete,
trop ai faich lonc badatge.

Ai bels amics, sivals un bel semblan
mi faitz enan
qu'ieu moira de dolor,
que.l amador
vos tenon per salvatge;
car joja non m'ave
de vos don no.m recre
d'amar per bona fe
totz temps ses cor volatge.

Mas ja vas vos non aurai cor truan
ni plen d'engan –
si tot vos m'ai pejor,
qu'a gran honor
m'o teing en mon coratge;
ans pens, quan mi sove
del ric pretz que.us mante,
e sai ben que.us cove
dompna d'aussor paratge.

II

God knows I should have had my fill of song –
the more I sing
the worse I fare in love,
and tears and cares
make me their home;
I've placed my heart and soul
in jeopardy,
and if I don't end this poem now
it will already be too long.

Oh handsome friend, just once before I die
of grief, show me
your handsome face;
the other lovers say
you are a beast –
but still, though no joy
comes to me from you,
I'm proud to love you always
in good faith, with an unfickle heart.

Nor ever from me a treacherous heart
toward you will turn –
though I be your inferior,
in loving I excel;
this I believe,
and this I think
even when I ponder your great worth,
and I know well that you deserve
a lady higher born that I.

Despois vos vi, ai fag vostre coman,
et anc per tan,
amics, no.us n'aic meillor;
que prejador
no.m mandetz ni messatge,
que ja.m viretz lo fre,
amics, non fassatz re:
car jois non mi soste,
ab pauc de dol non ratge.

Si pro i agues, be.us membri' en chantan
qu'aic vostre gan
qu'emblei ab gran temor;
pois aic paor
que i aguessetz dampnatge
d'aicella que.us rete,
amics, per qu'ieu desse
lo tornei, car ben cre
qu'ieu non ai poderatge.

Dels cavalliers conosc que i fan lor dan,
quar ja prejan
dompnas plus qu'ellas lor,
qu'autra ricor
noi an ni seignoratge;
que pois dompna s'ave
d'amar, prejar deu be
cavallier, s'en lui ve
proez' e vassalatge.

Dompna na Mieils, ancse
am so don mals mi ve,
car cel qui pretz mante
a vas mi cor volatge.

Since I first caught sight of you I've been
at your command; and yet, friend,
it's brought me naught,
for you've sent neither
messages nor envoys.
And if you left me now,
I wouldn't feel a thing,
for since no joy sustains me
a little pain won't drive me mad.

If it would do me any good, I'd remind you singing
that I had your glove –
I stole it trembling;
then I was afraid
you might get scolded
by the girl who loves you now:
so I gave it back fast, friend,
for I know well enough
that I am powerless.

Knights there are I know who harm themselves
in courting ladies
more than ladies them,
when they are neither
higher born nor richer;
for when a lady's mind
is set on love, she ought
to court the man, if he shows strength and chivalry.

Lady Almucs,* I always
love what's worst for me,
for he who's most deserving
has the heart most fleeting.

---

* Unknown reference. Castelloza could not have known Almucs de Castelnau, who died
ca. 1180 (see p. 93).

Bels Noms, ges no.m recre
de vos amar jasse,
car viu en bona fe,
bontatz e ferm coratge.

III

Mout avetz faich long estatge,
amics, pois de mi.us partitz,
et es me greu e salvatge,
quar me juretz e.m plevitz
que als jorns de vostra vida
non acsetz dompna mas me;
e si d'autra vos perte,
m'avetz morta e trahida,
qu'avi' en vos m'esperanssa
que m'amassetz ses doptanssa.

Bels amics, de fin coratge
vos amei, pois m'abellitz,
e sai que faich ai follatge,
que plus m'en etz escaritz;
qu'anc non fis vas vos ganchida,
e si.m fasetz mal per be:
be.us am e non m'en recre,
mas tan m'a amors sazida
qu'ieu non cre que benananssa
puosc' aver ses vostr' amanssa.

Good Name,* my love for you
will never cease,
for I live on kindness,
faith and constant courage.

III

You stayed a long time, friend,
and then you left me,
and it's a hard, cruel thing you've done;
for you promised and you swore
that as long as you lived
I'd be your only lady:
if now another has your love
you've slain me and betrayed me,
for in you lay all my hopes
of being loved without deceit.

Handsome friend, as a lover true
I loved you, for you pleased me,
but now I see I was a fool,
for I've barely seen you since.
I never tried to trick you,
yet you returned me bad for good;
I love you so, without regret,
but love has stung me with such force
I think no good can possibly
be mine unless you say you love me.

---

* A *senhal*.

Mout aurai mes mal usatge
a las autras amairitz,
qu'om sol trametre messatge
emotz triatz e chausitz:
e ieu tenc me per garida,
amics, a la mia fe,
quan vos prec, qu'aissi.m cove;
que.l plus pros n'es enriquida
s'a de vos qualqu' aondanssa
de baisar o d'acoindanssa.

Mal aj' ieu, s'anc cor volatge
vos aic ni.us fui camjairitz,
ni drutz de negun paratge
per me non fo encobitz;
anz sui pensiv' e marrida
car de m'amor no.us sove,
e si de vos jois no.m ve,
tost me trobaretz fenida:
car per pauc de malananssa
mor dompna, s'om tot no.il lanssa.

Tot lo maltraich e.l dampnatge
que per vos m'es escaritz
vos fai grazir mos linhatge
e sobre totz mos maritz;
e s'anc fetz vas me faillida,
perdon la.us per bona fe,
e prec que venhatz a me,
despois quez auretz auzida
ma chanson, que.us fatz fionsa:
sai trobetz bella semblansa.

I would have compared poorly
with the other women in your life,
for it's proper to send words
and messages selected with great care:
but I'm content, friend, by my faith,
to speak to you in person –
it suits me best;
for even highborn women are enriched
if from you they have some show
of kisses or affection.

May evil strike me down if ever
I was fickle or displayed
a flighty heart, or ever
wanted any other lover;
no, if I'm sad and mournful
it's because you don't remember me.
And if still I have no joy from you,
you'll soon come upon me dead:
for when unhappiness persists
a woman dies, unless her man speeds joy.

All the abuse and suffering
that's been my lot because of you
have made my family adore you,
and my husband most of all;*
and if you ever did me wrong
I pardon you in all good faith
and beg you to come back to me
now that you've heard my song:
for here, I promise you,
you'll find a fine reception.

---

* That is, suffering has made her write poems, which brings fame to her family.

Clara d'Anduza
fl. first half of 13th century

En greu esmai et en greu pessamen
an mes mon cor et en granda error
li lauzengier e.l fals devinador,
abaissador de joi e de joven;
quar vos qu'ieu am mais que res qu'el mon sia
an fait de me departir e lonhar,
si qu'ieu no.us puesc vezer ni remirar,
don muer de dol, d'ira e de feunia.

Cel que.m blasma vostr' amor ni.m defen
non pot en far en re mon cor meillor,
ni.l dous dezir qu'ieu ai de vos major
ni l'enveja ni.l dezir ni.l talen;
e non es om, tan mos enemics sia,
si.l n'aug dir ben, que non lo tenh' en car,
e, si 'n ditz mal, mais no.m pot dir ni far
neguna re que a plazer me sia.

Ja no.us donetz, bels amics, espaven
que ja ves vos aja cor trichador,
ni qu'ie.us camge per nul autr' amador;
qu'amors que.m te per vos en sa bailia
vol que mon cor vos estui e vos gar,
e farai o; e s'ieu pogues emblar
mon cor, tals l'a que jamais non l'auria.

Amics, tan ai d'ira e de feunia
quar no vos vey, que quan ieu cug chantar,
planh e sospir, per qu'ieu non puesc so far
ab mas coblas que.l cors complir volria.

Anduze was one of the most important towns in Languedoc.
CLARA D'ANDUZA *was probably the wife or daughter of*
Bernard d'Anduze, lord of the town.

The *lauzengiers* and the deceitful spies,
those diminishers of youth and joy,
have weighed my heart with cares and suffering,
have made it heavy with unending sighs;
for you whom I love more than anything
they've banished from my side,
and since I have no hope of seeing you again,
I die of grief, of anger and resentment.

Whoever blames my love for you or bans it
is powerless to help my heart improve
or to increase my love for you,
or my longing, my desire or my need.
And there's not a man I won't hold dear
for praising you, even an enemy,
but whoever speaks a word against you
can do nothing to regain my favor.

And you mustn't worry, handsome friend,
that I'd do anything to trick you,
or ever trade you for another man,
though a hundred suitors seek my hand;
for the love that has me in its spell
wants me to lock you up and guard you well;
and I will; and if I could remove my heart,
there's someone now from whom it would depart.

Friend, I'm so angry and resentful
from not seeing you that when I try to sing
I weep and sigh; and I can't make music
with the strophes that my heart is willing to supply.

Bieiris de Romans
first half of the 13th century?

Na Maria, pretz e fina valors,
e.l joi e.l sen e la fina beutatz,
e l'aculhir e.l pretz e las onors,
e.l gent parlar e l'avinen solatz,
e la dous car' e la gaja cuendansa,
e.l dous esgart e l'amoros semblan
que son en vos, don non avetz engansa,
me fan traire vas vos ses cor truan.

Per que vos prec, si.us platz que fin' amors
e gausiment e dous umilitatz
me posca far ab vos tan de socors,
que mi donetz, bella domna, si.us platz,
so don plus ai d'aver joi e 'speransa;
car en vos ai mon cor e mon talan,
e per vos ai tot so qu'ai d'alegransa
e per vos vauc mantas vetz sospiran.

E car beutatz e valor vos enansa
sobra totas, qu'una no.us es denan,
vos prec, si.us platz, per so que.us es onransa,
que non ametz entendidor truan.

Bella domna, cui pretz e joi enansa
e gen parlar, a vos mas coblas man,
car en vos es gajess' e alegranssa,
e tot lo ben qu'om en domna deman.

Nothing at all is known about BIEIRIS DE ROMANS *except her birthplace. Romans, northeast of Montélimar, produced another troubadour, Folquet de Romans, who flourished in the first half of the thirteenth century. This* chanson *is addressed to another woman, named Maria, whose identity is unknown.*

Lady Maria, in you merit and distinction,
joy, intelligence and perfect beauty,
hospitality and honor and distinction,
your noble speech and pleasing company,
your sweet face and merry disposition,
the sweet look and the loving expression
that exist in you without pretension
cause me to turn toward you with a pure heart.

Thus I pray you, if it please you that true love
and celebration and sweet humility
should bring me such relief with you,
if it please you, lovely woman, then give me
that which most hope and joy promises
for in you lie my desire and my heart
and from you stems all my happiness,
and because of you I'm often sighing.

And because merit and beauty raise you high
above all others (for none surpasses you),
I pray you, please, by this which does you honor,
don't grant your love to a deceitful suitor.

Lovely woman, whom joy and noble speech uplift,
and merit, to you my stanzas go,
for in you are gaiety and happiness,
and all good things one could ask of a woman.

Guillelma de Rosers
fl. mid-13th century

Na Guillelma, man cavalier arratge
anan de nueig, per mal temps que fasia,
si plagnian d'alberc en lor lengatge;
auziron o dui, qui per drudaria
s'en anavan vers lur domnas non len;
l'us s'en tornet per servir cella gen,
l'autres anet vers sa domna corren;
quals d'aquels dos fes miels so que.l tagnia?

Amics Lanfrancs, miels complit son viatge,
al meu semblan, cel que tenc vers s'amia;
e l'autres fes ben, mas son fin coratge
non poc saber tan ben sidonz a tria
com cil que.l vi denan sos oils presen,
qu'atendut l'ac sos cavalliers conven:
e val trop mais qui so que dis aten
que qui en als son coratge cambia.

Domna, si.us platz, tot quan fes d'agradatge
lo cavalliers que par sa gaillardia
garda.ls autres de mort e de damnatge
li moc d'amor; que ges de cortezia
non a nuls oms, si d'amor no.l deisen:
per que sidons deu.l grazir per un cen,
car deslivret per s'amor de turmen
tanz cavaliers, que se vista l'avia.

GUILLELMA DE ROSERS *was probably from Rougiers, near Monaco,
on what is now the Côte d'Azur. She exchanged this tenson
with Lanfrancs Cigala, a lawyer-troubadour from Genoa.*

Dame Guillelma, several knights travelling by dark,
despondent, in the worst of weather,
wished aloud in their own tongue for a place to stay;
these were overheard by two lovers on their way
to see their ladies in the neighborhood;
one of them turned back to help the gentlemen,
the other one ran straight on to his lady:
which of them did as he should?

Friend Lanfrancs, as I see it he did best
who continued toward his lady; the other one
also did well, but his lady couldn't tell
the way the other could, who saw
with her own eyes her lover's worth,
for she kept waiting for her lover to arrive:
a man who keeps his word is worth much more
than one whose plans are constantly revised.

Excuse me, lady, but it was love
that moved the knight who by his courage saved
the rest from death and harm – there's no such thing
as chivalry that doesn't spring from love;
thus, in my opinion, his lady ought
to thank him hundredfold, as if she'd seen his deed
with her own eyes, for out of love of her
he rescued all those knights from injury.

Lanfrancs, jamais non razonetz musatge
tan gran quan fon d'aicel qu'aisso fasia,
quar sapchatz ben, mout i fes gran oltratge;
pois bels servirs tan de cor li movia,
car non servi sidons premieiramen?
et agra 'n grat d'ell' e dels eissamen,
pois per s'amor pogra servir soven
en mans bos locs, que faillir noi podia.

Merce vos quier, domna, s'ieu dic follatge;
qu'oimais vei so que tot o mescrezia:
que non vos plai qu'autre pelegrinatge
fassan li drut mas vers vos tota via;
pero cavals qu'om vol que biort gen
deu om menar ab mesur' et ab sen,
e car los drutz cochatz tan malamen,
lur faill poders, don vos sobra feunia.

Ancar vos dic que son malvatz usatge
degra laissar en aquel mezeis dia
li cavalliers, pois domna d'aut paratge
bella e pros dec aver en baillia;
qu'en son alberc servion largamen,
ja el no.i fos; mas chascuns razon pren,
quar el si sen tan de recrezemen
qu'al major ops poders li failliria.

Domna, poder ai ieu et ardimen,
non contra vos que venses en jazen,
per qu'ieu fui fols car ab vos pris conten,
mas vencut voill que m'ajatz, com que sia.

Lanfrancs, aitan vos autrei e.us consen
que tan mi sent de cor e d'ardimen
qu'ab aital geing com domna si defen
mi defendri' al plus ardit que sia.

Lanfrancs, you've never tried to justify
such absurd behavior as this man's,
for you know well he acted very badly;
if he was so moved as you say by chivalry,
why didn't he first serve his lady?
Both she and they'd have thanked him equally,
and there's no lack of opportunity
to serve, in places where there's much less risk.

Forgive me, lady, for speaking foolishly.
Now I see that my suspicions all along were true,
that you can't be content unless
all lovers' pilgrimages lead to you;
but if you want to teach a horse to joust,
you have to guide it with intelligence and care,
and since you urge them on so hard, the lovers
lose their strength, and you end up enraged.

I'll tell you once again,
that man should change his attitude
that very day, and swear allegiance
to a lady noble, beautiful and rich.
Besides, in his own house they would have served
an ample meal, even if he wasn't there;
they all claim to be right, but he feels so contrite
that in a real emergency he'd be unnerved.

Lady, I have strength and pertinacity
(not for you whom I can beat supine –
and what a fool I was for loving you that time),
but, by any means available, I challenge you to conquer me.

Lanfrancs, I promise and I guarantee
that I'm so strong in feeling and tenacity
that with a woman's subtlety
I'll ward off the most covetous design.

Domna H.

Rosin, digatz m'ades de cors
cals fetz meills, car etz conoissens:
una domna coind' e valens
que ieu sai, a dos amadors,
e vol qu'usquecs jur e pliva
enans que.ls vuoill' ab si colgar
que plus mas tener e baisar
no.lh faran; e l'uns s'abriva
el faig, que sagramen no.lh te,
l'autres no.l ausa far per re.

Domna, d'aitan sobret follors
cel que fon desobedïens
ves sidons, que non es parvens
qu'amans, pois lo destreing amors,
dej' ab voluntat forciva
los ditz de sa domna passar;
per qu'ieu dig que senes cobrar
deu perdre la joj' autiva
de sidons cel qui frais la fe,
e l'autres deu trobar merce.

A fin amic non tol paors,
Rosin, de penre jauzimens,
que.l dezirs e.l sobretalans
lo destreng tan que per clamors
de sidons nominativa
noi.s pot soffrir ni capdellar,
qu'ab jazer et ab remirar
l'amors corals recaliva
tan fort que non au ni non ve
ni conois quan fai mal o be.

Nothing at all is known about her. Rosin is a senhal, *and
offers no clue about the origin of this* tenson.

Rosin, tell me from the heart
which one did best, for you're an expert.
I know a lady who's both charming
and distinguished, who has two lovers.
And she wants each of them to swear
and pledge, before she'll let him near,
that he's not planning to do more
than hug or kiss her; one immediately
does it, for oaths are meaningless to him;
the other doesn't dare.

Lady, the one who disobeyed
his lady was a fool,
for when a man is in love's grip
it's wrong for him to knowingly
ignore his lady's orders.
Thus in all honesty I'd say
the one who broke his lady's faith
should lose her solemn joy:
the other one deserves her grace.

Rosin, fear shouldn't keep
a courtly lover from
experiencing joy,
where zeal and passion bind him so
that he can neither suffer nor forego
his sovereign lady's
voice; for shared bed and lovely sight
make true love turn so bright
that he can't hear or see or know
if he does wrong or right.

Domna, ben mi par grans errors
d'amic, pois ama coralmens,
que nuills gaug li sia plazens
qu'a sa domna non si' onors;
car no.lh deu esser esquiva
pena per sa domna onrar,
ni.l deu res per dreg agradar,
s'a leis non es agradiva:
e drutz qu'enaissi no.s capte
deu perdre sa domna e se.

Rosins, dels crois envazidors
aunitz e flacs e recrezens
sapchatz que fon l'aunitz dolens
que se perdet en meig del cors;
mas l'arditz on pretz s'aviva
saup gen sa valor enansar,
quan pres tot so que.lh fon plus car
mentre.lh fon l'amors aiziva:
e domna qu'aital drut mescre
mal creira cel qui s'en recre.

Domna, sapchatz que grans valors
fon de l'amic e chauzimens
que.l fetz gardar de falhimens
esperan de sidons socors,
e cel fetz foudat nadiva
que sa domna auset forsar,
e que.l mante sap pauc d'amar;
qu'amans, pois fin' amors viva
lo destreing tan, sa domna.l cre
de tot quan ditz, qu'aissi.s cove.

Lady, it seems to me a lover
errs, if he sincerely loves,
in finding pleasing any joy
that honors not his lady;
for the honor of his lady ought never
to be arduous to him,
nor ever bring him pleasure anything
that she would not find pleasing:
the lover who neglects these rules
deserves to lose his lady and himself.

Rosin, of the invaders cruel
and weak and cowardly and shamed,
know this: it was the shameful sad one
who lost his way mid-course;
but the courageous one whose valor shines
knew how to augment his esteem,
for he took what was most dear to him
the moment love made him feel welcome:
she who disbelieves a lover such as him
won't easily believe a weakling.

Lady, that lover possessed valor
and discretion who kept guard
against transgression in the hope
of being rescued by his lady;
the one who dared to force her will
was a complete fool.
Ignorant of love are his defenders;
for when a lover's in the grip
of perfect love, he believes
his lady's every word: thus should it be.

Oimais conosc ben cossi va,
Rosin, pois que.us aug encolpar
lo fin e.l caitiu razonar;
qu'eissamens obra caitiva
fariatz, e midons desse
n'Agnesina diga qu'en cre.

De mi non cal qu'ieu o pliva,
que.l ver en podetz ben triar,
domna, si.us platz; e mout m'es car:
que midons on pretz s'aviva
n'Agnesina demand ab se
na Cobeitosa de tot be.

Now I understand, Rosin,
exactly how it works, since I hear you
blame the good man and defend the bad:
just the same, you'd commit
a crime, and let my lady
Agnesina* say what she may.

It's all the same to me
if I swear or not, for you're quite
capable of finding out the truth;
but I'm glad my lady
Agnesina, in whom all worth resides,
has sent Lady Cupidity* away.

---

* Neither of these references is clear. Both *tornadas* seem to refer to a specific situation, but their meaning is hidden in *trobar clus*.

Alais, Iselda and Carenza

Na Carenza al bel cors avinen,
donatz conseil a nos doas serors,
e car sabetz meils triar lo meillors,
conseillatz mi segon vostr' escïen:
penrai marit a nostra conoissenza?
o starai mi pulcela? e si m'agensa,
que far filhos no cug que sia bos;
essems maritz mi par trop angoissos.

Na Carenza, penre marit m'agenza,
mas far enfantz cug qu'es grans penedenza,
que las tetinhas pendon aval jos
e.l ventrilhs es cargatz e enojos.

N'Alais i na Iselda, ensenhamen,
pretz e beltat, joven, frescas colors
conosc qu'avetz, cortez' e valors
sobre totas las autras conoissen;
per qu'ie.us conseil per far bona semenza
penre marit Coronat de Scienza,
en cui faretz fruit de filh glorïos:
retengud' es pulcel' a qui l'espos.

N'Alais i na Iselda, sovinenza
ajatz de mi, i lumbra de ghirenza;
quan i seretz, prejatz lo glorïos
qu'al departir mi retenga pres vos.

*Nothing is known about any of these three women. The poem is
a strange mixture of colloquial and religious language, and much
of it remains obscure.*

Lady Carenza of the lovely, gracious body,
give some advice to us two sisters,
and since you know best how to tell what's best,
counsel me according to your own experience:
shall I marry someone we both know?
or shall I stay unwed? that would please me,
for making babies doesn't seem so good,
and it's too anguishing to be a wife.

Lady Carenza, I'd like to have a husband,
but making babies I think is a huge penitence:
your breasts hang way down
and it's too anguishing to be a wife

Lady Alais and Lady Iselda,
you have learning, merit, beauty, youth, fresh
color, courtly manners and distinction
more than all the other women that I know;
I therefore advise you, if you want to plant good seed,
to take as a husband Coronat de Scienza,*
from whom you shall bear as fruit glorious sons:
saved is the chastity of her who marries him.

Lady Alais and Lady Iselda, may memory
of me shine as your protection;
and when you get there, pray the King of Glory
that when I leave he place me by your side.†

---

* Perhaps a Cathar (or Gnostic) name for Christ; in any case, the message seems to be
that marriage with God – "Crowned With Knowledge" – is more desirable than
marriage with a human man.
† These four lines are "closed" enough to qualify as *trobar clus.*

Anonymous I

Amics, en gran cossirier
sui per vos et en greu pena,
e del mal qu'ieu en suffier
non cre que vos sentatz guaire;
doncs, per que.us metetz amaire,
pus a me laissatz tot lo mal?
quar abdui no.l partem egual?

Domna, amors a tal mestier,
pus dos amics encadena,
que.l mal qu'an e l'alegrier
senta quecs a son vejaire;
qu'ieu pens, e non sui guabaire,
que la dura dolor coral
ai ieu tota a mon cabal.

Amics, s'acsetz un cartier
de la dolor que.m malmena,
be viratz mon encombrier;
mas no.us cal del mieu dan guaire,
que quan no m'en puesc estraire,
com que m'an, vos es cominal,
an me be o mal atretal.

Domna, quar ist lauzengier
que m'an tout sen e alena
son nostr' anguoissos guerrier,
lais m'en, non per talan vaire,
quar no.us sui pres, qu'ab lor braire
nos an bastit tal joc mortal
que non jauzem jauzen jornal.

This tenson *between a man and woman was formerly attributed to the Countess of Dia and Raimbaut d'Orange.*

Friend, because of you I'm filled
with grievous sorrow and despair,
but I doubt you feel a trace
of my affliction.
Why did you become a lover,
since you leave the suffering to me?
Why don't we split it evenly?

Lady, such is love's nature
when it links two friends together,
that whatever grief or joy they have
each feels according to his way.
The way I see it, and I don't
exaggerate, all the worst pain's
been on my end of the game.

Friend, if you felt a quarter
of the anguish that torments me,
you'd understand my woes,
but you don't seem to care at all;
and though I can't do anything
about it, to you it's all the same
whether I fare well or ill.

Lady, it's the *lauzengiers* –
our spiteful enemies – who've robbed
my breath and sanity;
because of them, not lack of love,
I don't come near. They've set a deadly trap,
for thanks to their infernal noise,
we can't enjoy our daily joy.

Amics, nulh grat no.us refier
quar ja.l mieus dans vos refrena
de vezer me que.us enquier;
e si vos faitz plus guardaire
del mieu dan qu'ieu non vuelh faire,
be.us tenc per sobreplus lejal
que no son cilh de l'espital.

Domna, ieu tem a sobrier
qu'aur perda, e vos arena,
que per dig de lauzengier
nostr' amors torne s'en caire;
per so deg tener en guaire
trop plus que vos, per sanh Marsal,
quar etz la res que mais me val.

Amics, tan vos sai leugier
en fait d'amorosa mena
qu'ieu cug que de cavalier
siatz devengutz camjaire;
e deg vos o be retraire,
quar be paretz que pessetz d'al,
pus del mieu pessamen no.us cal.

Domna, jamais esparvier
non port, ni cas ab cerena,
s'anc pus que.m detz joi entier
fui de nulh' autra enquistaire;
ni non sui aitals bauzaire –
mas per enveja.l deslial
m'o alevon e.m fan venal.

Friend, your pains will get no thanks from me,
for the risks I run should not prevent
your visits to the one who loves you so;
if you insist on fretting more than I
about my reputation,
then I'll say that you're more loyal
than the good knights of the Hospital.*

Lady, what has me terrified
is that I'll lose my gold and you your sand,†
that the words of *lauzengiers*
could undermine a love like ours.
Thus, more than you, I should watch out,
for, by Saint Martial,†† you're the thing
most precious to me in the world.

Friend, I know well enough how skilled
you are in amorous affairs,
and I find you rather changed
from the chivalrous knight you used
to be. I might as well be clear,
for your mind seems quite distracted:
do you still find me attractive?

Lady, may sparrow-hawk not ride
my wrist, nor siren fly beside
me on the chase, if ever
since you gave me perfect joy
I possessed another woman;
I don't lie: out of envy
evil men insult my name.

---

* Crusading order that flourished in the 12th century in Palestine. Like the Templars,
the Hospitaliers (Knights of St. John) were known for their religious zeal and chivalrous
good works.
† A mixed conceit; by making her gold and himself sand, he praises her and
deprecates himself.
†† Patron saint of prisoners (prisoners of love?).

Amics, creirai vos per aital
qu'aissi.us aja totz temps lejal.

Domna, aissi m'auretz lejal:
que jamais non pensarai d'al.

Friend, I'd happily believe you
if you'd be forever faithful.

Lady, you shall have me faithful:
henceforth I'll think exclusively of you.

Anonymous II

Bona domna, tan vos ai fin coratge
non puesc mudar no.us cosselh vostre be:
e dic vos be que faitz gran vilanatge,
car cel ome qu'anc tan non amet re
laissatz morir e non sabetz per que;
pero, si mor, vostre er lo damnatge,
qu'autra domna mas vos a grat no.l ve,
ni en lui non a poder ni senhoratge.

Na donzela, be.m deu esser salvatge
quan el gaba ni.se vana de me;
tan a son cor fol e leu a volatge
que m'amistat en lunha re no.s te:
per que m'amors no.l tanh ni no.l cove,
e pus el eis s'a enques lo folatge,
non m'en reptatz si la foldatz l'en ve,
qu'aissi aug dir que dretz es e onratge.

Bona domna, ardre.l podetz o pendre,
o far tot so que.us venga a talen,
que res non es qu'el vos puesca defendre:
aissi l'avetz ses tot retenemen;
e no.m par ges que.us sia d'avinen,
pus ab un bais li fetz lo cor estendre
aissi co.l focs que.l mort carbon encen –
pueis, quan el mor, no vo'n cal merce pendre.

This anonymous tenson *between a married woman and a* doncela
is an interesting variation on the theme of the tenson *between
Almucs and Iseut, p. 92.*

Good lady, so deeply do I care for you
that I can't keep from giving you advice.
I tell you, you're committing a grave crime,
for, without knowing why, you're letting die
a man who never cherished anything so much;
and if he dies, it's you who'll be to blame,
for you're the only woman he'll consent to see:
you alone have power over him and sovereignty.

Maiden, I have every reason to be cruel
if he brags and boasts about me:
he's so lighthearted and fickle, such a fool,
that he can't even manage to sustain our dalliance
and since my love seems not to fit his plans,
and he himself has sought out madness,
don't reproach me if I take offense,
for I've heard said that it's both right and common sense.

Good lady, you can have him burned or hanged
or do whatever strikes your fancy,
for there's nothing he can do to stop you,
since you're holding him so ruthlessly;
but I don't think it's very kind of you,
since with a single kiss you'd make his heart expand
the way a flame spreads fire through dead wood;
and once he's dead, it's useless to forgive.

Na donzela, non m'en podetz rependre,
que.l deg m'amor ab aital covinen
que el fos mieus per donar e per vendre
e que totz temps fos a mon mandamen;
mas el a fag vas me tal falhimen
don ges no.s pot escondir ni defendre:
non o fatz mal si m'amor li defen,
car ja per el non vuelh mon pretz dissendre.

Süau parlem, domna, qu'om no.us entenda:
ara digatz, que forfaitz es vas vos,
mais que per far vostres plazers se renda
son cor umil contra.l vostr' ergulhos.
Vuelh que.m digatz, domna, per cals razos
poiretz estar que merces non vo.n prenda,
que mil sospirs ne fa.l jorn angoissos,
don per un sol no.l denhatz far esmenda.

Si m'amor vol, na donzela, que renda,
ben li er obs que sia gais e pros,
francs et umils, qu'ab nulh om no.s contenda
e a cascun sia de bel respos;
qu'a me non tanh om fel ni ergulhos
per que mon pretz dechaja ni dissenda,
mas francs e fis, celans et amoros:
s'el vol que.l don lezer que mi entenda.

Aital l'auretz, ja regart non vo.n prenda,
bona domna, que.l sieu cor avetz vos;
que el non a poder qu'ad autr' entenda.

Bonis la fin, donzela, ab que s'atenda;
e vos siatz garda entre nos dos,
e que.us tengatz ab aquel que.l tort prenda.

Maiden, I can't understand your rationale:
I granted him my love on the condition
he'd be mine to give away or sell,
and that he'd always be at my command;
but he's wronged me so gravely
that he barely knows where he should hide;
no, I haven't erred if I've deprived him of my love:
and I won't ever lower myself for his sake.

Let's speak softly lady, let no one overhear;
you say, since the wrong was done to you,
that to please you he should break
his humble heart against your proud one.
Now I want to know, lady, in your own words,
how it is that you're untouched by pity
when he sighs a thousand times each tortured day:
why not a single sigh can make you make amends.

Maiden, if he really wants my love,
he'll have to show high spirits and behave,
be frank and humble, not pick fights with any man,
be courteous with everyone;
for I don't want a man who's proud or bitter,
who'll debase my worth or ruin me,
but one who's frank and noble, loving and discreet:
this let him hear if he wants leniency.

So shall you have him, lady, if regret betray
you not, for his heart belongs to you;
and it won't change, though his love remain unpaid.

The ending's happy, maiden, if we're not waylaid:
let you be guardian between us two,
and stay beside whichever goes astray.

Anonymous III

I

Si.m fos grazitz mos chanz ieu m'esforzera
e dera.m gaug e deportz e solatz,
mas aissi.m sui a non-chaler gitatz
que ma dompna, que a totz jorns esmera
so qu'ieu li dic, non deign' en grat tener;
qu'apenas sai entre.ls pros remaner,
ni no.m sui ges cel que era antan:
aissi me tol mos covinenz e.ls fran.

Ailas! cum muor quan mi membra cum era
gais e joves, alegres, envesatz!
e quan m'albir qu'ieu sui de joi loignatz,
per pauc mos cors del tot no.s desespera;
e donc mei oill cum la poiran vezer,
quar n'ai perdut d'els e de mi poder?
so m'an ill fag, don mos cors vai ploran,
que no.n posc far conort ni bel semblan.

Ai! bella dompna, res cum be.m semblera
que, on que fos, degues umilitatz
venser en vos que tan umils semblatz
vers mi que ja a mos jornz no.s camjera
amors en tort, que.us fai dur cor aver;
e vos sabetz, quar l'en donatz poder –
quar si amors e vos es a mon dan,
las! ges longuas non posc soffrir l'affan.

This tenson *breaks the usual pattern of alternating stanzas;*
part I is in the voice of a man, part II that of a woman.

I

I'd be encouraged if I liked what I compose,
for I'd feel joy and satisfaction and repose,
but I'm so hopelessly distracted
that my lady, who must constantly improve
the things I write to her, won't deign approval.
I barely know how to keep my place
among the men, for I'm not what I once was:
she takes my precious covenant and breaks it.

Oh, how I die when I remember how I was
when I was young and gay, spontaneous and joyful;
and when I realize how I've strayed from joy
my heart all but gives way to desperation:
how shall my eyes gaze at her now,
when they and I have lost our strength?
That's what she's done to me, why my heart weeps,
and no consolation's to be found.

Ah, lovely lady, how happy I would be
if, no matter where I was, I could conquer
your humility, you who seem so meek
toward me who on my life would never
change my love to make your heart grow hard;
and you know what I mean, for you believe it,
but if love and you will do me harm,
alas! I can't go on with this for long.

II

Bels douz amics, ja de mi no.s clamera
vostre bels cors cortes et enseignatz
si saubessetz cals es ma voluntatz:
vos es de cui sui mielz hoi que non era:
e non creatz que.us met' en non-chaler,
quar gaug entier non posc ses vos aver
a cui m'autrei lejalmen ses enjan:
e.us lais mon cor en gatge, on qu'ieu m'an.

Mas una gens enojosa e fera,
cui gautz ni bes ni alegrers non platz,
nos guerrejan, dan mos cors es iratz,
quar per ren als senes vos non estera;
per so en mi avetz tan de poder
qu'ab vos venrai quan mi.l faretz saber,
mal grat de cels qu'enqueron nostre dan:
e pesa.m fort quar ses vos estauc tan.

II

If you knew my mind, sweet handsome friend,
your handsome noble learned heart
no longer would lament; for you're the one
who's made me happier today than ever.
And don't think I'm indifferent:
to me true joy's impossible without you
to whom I give myself sincerely.
Wherever I go, you have my heart in guarantee.

A certain cruel, annoying crew,*
opposed to joy and bliss and kisses,
wars against us, which brings anger to my heart;
for I refuse to live without you.
That's why you've such power over me
that I'll come running when you call,
despite those men who seek our fall.
And it grieves me that we've been so long apart.

---

* i.e., the *lauzengiers.*

BIOGRAPHIES

IN THE jungle of information about the human race that now exists, the traces of medieval women are decidely faint. The accumulation of records since the invention of the printing press has created monumental archives stuffed with charters, deeds, wills and insurance policies which only passion or obsession would lead anyone to read. In this book, it was my obsession to seek out every possible clue to the existence of the women troubadours which led me to examine endless genealogies, dictionaries of heraldry and assorted accounts of noble families of Occitania – all extraordinarily obscure, dusty, and often, it must be said, boring. Here and there, always attached to the name of a male relative, the name of a woman troubadour appeared out of the gloom.

The biographies which follow are the result of this research. It is in the ardent hope of sparing others the travail required for the unearthing of each single fact that they are printed here in all their glorious detail.

MANUSCRIPT SOURCES

Following Bartsch:

A	Rome	Biblioteca Vaticana 5232
B	Paris	Bibliothèque Nationale Fr. 1592
C	Paris	Bibliothèque Nationale Fr. 856
D	Modena	Biblioteca Estense a, R, 4, 4
d	Modena	appendage to D
F	Rome	Biblioteca Chigiana L.IV.106
H	Rome	Biblioteca Vaticana 3207
I	Paris	Bibliothèque Nationale Fr. 854
K	Paris	Bibliothèque Nationale Fr. 12473
M	Paris	Bibliothèque Nationale Fr. 12474
N	New York	Morgan Library 819
N^2	Berlin	Staatsbibliothek, Phillips 1910
O	Rome	Biblioteca Vaticana 3208
Q	Florence	Biblioteca Riccardiana 2909
R	Paris	Bibliothèque Nationale Fr. 22543
T	Paris	Bibliothèque Nationale Fr. 15211

Sources for both poems and *vidas* are given in the biographies, which are arranged in chronological order. Except where otherwise indicated, the chief source for the poetic texts is Oscar Schultz-Gora's *Die Provenzalischen Dichterinnen*, Leipzig, 1888. The *vidas* are to be found in J. Boutière and A. Schultz, *Biographies des Troubadours*, Paris, 1964, abbreviated as Boutière. My immediate source is given first followed by the ms. source.

Tibors
Source of Poem: Schultz-Gora, p. 25; H

> *VIDA:*
> *Na Tibors was a lady of Provence, from a castle of En Blacatz*
> *called Sarenom. She was courtly and accomplished, gracious*
> *and very wise. And she knew how to write poems* (trobar). *And*
> *she fell in love and was fallen in love with, and was greatly honored*
> *by all the good men of that region, and admired and respected by all*
> *the worthy ladies . . . .*
>
> Boutière, p. 498; H

The life of Tibors is a good example of the difficulty of establish-
ing exact facts about the women troubadours. Although she is
one of the eight who are accorded a place in the *vidas,* her *vida*
provides little to go on. Tibors was a common name in Occitania
in the Middle Ages. But because of a happy coincidence which
seems to make her a sister of the troubadour Raimbaut d'Orange,
who has been studied in depth, we have access to a fair amount of
information on her. All this, of course, assuming that she is the
Tibors who was a sister of Raimbaut d'Orange. This same Tibors
was the wife of Bertrand des Baux, one of the major patrons of
the troubadours.

Walter T. Pattison's study of Raimbaut d'Orange[1] cites the
will of Raimbaut's mother, which provides the clue that links
the historical Tibors to the Tibors of the *vida.* It also permits us to
establish the essential dates of Tibors' life.

Raimbaut d'Orange was the son of Guilhem d'Omelas and
Tibors d'Orange, who held the title to the castle of Sarenom (now
Sérignan, near Grasse, Alpes Maritimes).[2] While it is possible
that she could have been the author of the poem on p. 81 and
the subject of the *vida,* it is far likelier that the *trobairitz* was one
of her two daughters, both of whom were named Tibors, after
the fashion of the time. Both of them lived at the height of
troubadour poetry, while the elder Tibors would have been a
bit on the early side. Of the two, the older sister is the more
probable candidate, since she was more closely connected with
her poet-brother.

Tibors' will is dated 1150, the date of her husband's marriage gift to Tiburgette, who by her name must be the younger of the two sisters. The will makes the elder Tibors guardian, along with her husband Bertrand des Baux, of Raimbaut d'Orange, who was still a minor. This daughter, according to Pattison, was the widow of Gaufroy de Mornas,[3] so we can assume that by 1150 she was in her second marriage. Pattison dates her parents' marriage 1129 or 1130; Tibors herself could not have been born much later than 1130 to be in her second marriage in 1150. Since girls were married in their early teens, it is conceivable that if she had been widowed almost immediately, and remarried as soon as a suitable husband could be found, she might have been born a few years later than 1130.

Bertrand des Baux, who was allied with Barcelona, was reportedly assassinated in 1181 on the order of his enemy, Raimon V of Toulouse.[4] Tibors died the following year, aged approximately fifty-two.[5] They had three sons.[6]

Countess of Dia

Source of Poems: I: Schultz-Gora, p. 17; CDI. II: Schultz-Gora, p. 18; A. III: Schultz-Gora, p. 18; A. IV: G. Kussler-Ratyé, "Les Chansons de la Comtesse de Die," Archiv. Rom., vol. I, t. l, p. 174; D.

> VIDA:
> The Countess of Dia was the wife of En Guillem de Poitiers, a lady beautiful and good. And she fell in love with En Raimbaut d'Orange, and wrote many good chansons in his honor.
>
> Boutière, p. 445, ABIK

All the dictionaries of heraldry and all the fat *recueils* of Gallic history and legend have not been able to yield up a satisfactory identity for the Countess of Dia. There are simply too many problems connected with her *vida*. Briefly, they are as follows. There is no wife of a Guillem de Poitiers who can be construed to have held title to the county of Die (today a small town northeast of Orange, *dép.* Drôme). There is, however, a Guillem of Poitiers, by legend a bastard offshoot of the great house of

Poitiers (Guilhem IX, Eleanor of Aquitaine, etc.), who was married to a lady of the Viennois whose *son* appears to have held the title Count of Dia.[7]

This woman was the daughter of Marguérite de Bourgogne Comté (d. 1163) and of Guigues IV, dauphin of the Viennois and Count of Albon, who died young on the battlefield in 1142, leaving Marguérite "desolate . . . with her twin daughters and infant son."[8] The Countess of Dia, it seems, may have been one of those twin daughters. The Guillem of Poitiers she married was a count; but his title was to Valentinois (which he passed on to their son Aymar) and not to Die. One possibility: since she was a countess both by virtue of her birth and through her marriage to Guillem, could she not have taken the name Countess of Dia subsequent to her son's assumption of the title in 1189?[9]

Raimbauts of Orange were a dime a dozen in the twelfth century and into the thirteenth, so there is little difficulty in showing that the Countess of Dia could have known one, particularly given the proximity of the two towns. If the Countess of Dia was in fact the wife of Guillem de Poitiers, Count of Valentinois, then the Raimbaut d'Orange who was her contemporary would have been the great troubadour himself, who lived from roughly 1146 to 1173.[10]

Raimbaut's older sister, Tibors, was also a poet. She and her husband Bertrand des Baux brought up the orphan Raimbaut at their court of Les Baux, a cultural center renowned for its patronage of troubadours. Les Baux is about the same distance from Avignon as Die is from Orange, and it is possible that Raimbaut and Tibors could have known the Countess of Dia. Then again, it is equally possible that their paths never crossed. The whole thing is speculation, and we must resign ourselves to the likelihood that we will never know anything more concrete.

There is no reason to believe a popular tradition that calls the Countess of Dia "Beatritz." In this case, however, the tradition would be upheld, since the wife of the Guillem de Poitiers described above was in fact named Beatritz.

Almucs de Castelnau and Iseut de Capio
Source of Poem: Schultz-Gora, p. 25; H

There is no *vida* for either of these two women, although they are given a long and useless *razo*. However, Anselme[11] provides a significant set of facts which gives us an Almodis of Caseneuve (the French equivalent of Castelnau) in the Vaucluse, some twenty miles east of Avignon. Less than ten miles away is Les Chapelins, certainly a possible derivation from Capio.

There are several reasons for accepting this identification of Almucs. The first is chronological; the second is the known connection of the Caseneuve lords with troubadours and troubadour poetry.

After the death of his first wife in 1152, Guiraut I de Simiane, lord of Caseneuve, Apt and Gordes, married Almodis (we know nothing of her family), with whom he had at least four sons – daughters are unmentioned in the chronicles unless they are sole heirs. A charter from 1173 shows that in that year he took the second son, Raimbaut (see below) on Crusade. Assuming that to undertake the journey the boy must have been at least ten years old at this time, then if he was born in 1163 his older brother could have been born in 1162 at the latest. Thus Almodis (Almucs) married no later than 1161, or very early in 1162. If, to be conservative, we assume that she was at least fourteen when she was married, she could not have been born later than 1147. To make a little leeway – since Guiraut, as a widower, would probably have remarried rather quickly after 1152 – I am inclined to see Almodis married by 1155 at the latest, and to place the date of her birth circa 1140, although she could have been born a good deal earlier.

Guiraut was a witness to the will of Tibors, the mother of Raimbaut d'Orange, who died in 1150. Thus he is at least ten years older than Almucs. And if he is the same Guiraut de Simiane who appears in acts of 1113 and 1120, he would be nearly thirty years older than she. This would mean that he made the journey to the Holy Land when he was well into his sixties. That is by no means impossible, since many people undertook the trip in the hope of dying there. Perhaps this was the case with Guiraut de Simiane, who arranged all his affairs before he left. In any case, it seems that both he and his wife were dead by 1184, the year in which the same second son Raimbaut made a grant of land to the Abbey of Sénanque in the name of his parents.

All these dates place Almucs, and by extension Iseut (about whom we know nothing independent of Almucs) squarely in the twelfth century, at the height of the so-called classical period of troubadour poetry. We know in addition that her son Raimbaut, who became known as Raimbaut d'Agoult, was an important patron of troubadours, and that he wrote some poems himself.[12] He is mentioned in twelve poems of Gaucelm Faidit as N'Agout:

> ... assuredly Raimon d'Agout, *seigneur* of Saut and the area of Apt between roughly 1170 and 1204. This important baron was the patron most prized by Gaucelm, and he protected him during the first part of his career. One of the poems refers to "Agout and his acquaintances," in other words, to a group of Provençal lords brought together by proximity, but no doubt also by friendship and by a shared love of courtly poetry ...[13]

All the more reason, then, to accept Almodis de Caseneuve as the Almucs de Castelnau of the poem.

Azalais de Porcairages
Source of Poem: Schultz-Gora, p. 16; CDHI

> *VIDA:*
> *Na Azalais de Porcairages was from the region of Montpellier, a noble and accomplished lady. And she fell in love with En Gui Guerrejat, who was the brother of En Guilhem de Montpellier. And she knew how to write poems, and she composed many good chansons in his honor.*
>
> *Boutière, p. 341; IK*

Clearly, the *vida* provides little concrete information about Azalais. If in general we trust the *vidas* on their geographical data – a risk which I think is worth taking – we find in the region of Montpellier the little town of Portiragnes, some five miles southeast of Béziers, in the Hérault.

From the one surviving poem by Azalais there are two additional clues: the allusion, in the *envoi* or *tornada,* to the illustrious countess Ermengarda of Narbonne, who we know reigned from 1143–1192; and the mention of Orange, undoubtedly a reference to a nobleman of that city. From the latter we are justified in *conjecturing* that Azalais is referring to the troubadour Raimbaut d'Orange, who had extensive holdings in the area around Montpellier and whom she could conceivably have known.[14] However, there is no reference to either Azalais or the town of Portiragnes in Raimbaut's *vida* or in the book-length study on him by Walter T. Pattison. [15]

Gui Guerrejat can be positively identified as the fifth son of Guillaume VI de Montpellier and brother of Guillaume VII. He died in 1177 and was buried in the Benedictine abbey of Valmagne – only ten miles from Portiragnes.[16]

Going simply by the dates, it is therefore possible that an Azalais of Porcairages/Portiragnes coincided in time with Ermengarda of Narbonne, Raimbaut d'Orange and Gui Guerrejat, and that she could have known all three of them.

It is also reasonable to suppose that Azalais was somewhat older than both Raimbaut and Gui, if indeed there was any sort of liaison between her and either of them. The ideal woman of courtly love was married and generally older than the man. For this reason I am inclined to place her birth not later than 1140 (Raimbaut d'Orange was born in 1146, according to Pattison).

We know from Pattison that Raimbaut died in 1173. But Azalais' poem is, to say the least, ambiguous. Is she mourning Raimbaut's death? If so, then we would date its composition around 1173. But if she is lamenting a betrayal or repudiation then we would have to place it somewhere between 1164 (the year Raimbaut would have been eighteen, a likely earliest age for him to be involved with Azalais) and 1173.

Maria de Ventadorn

Source of Poem: Schultz-Gora, p. 21; A

RAZO:

You have certainly heard of my lady Maria de Ventadorn, how she was the most sought-after lady there ever was in the Limousin, and the one who did most good and most kept herself from evil. And her good sense always helped her, and folly never made her do foolish things. And God honored her with a pretty, graceful body that was unequalled. En Gui d'Ussel had lost his lady, as you heard in the song which goes, "Si be.m partetz, mala dompna, de vos," on account of which he lived in great pain and in great sadness. And a long time had passed during which he neither sang nor composed, on account of which all the good ladies of that region were greatly grieved, and my lady Maria more than any, because En Gui d'Ussels used to praise her in all his songs. And the Count of the Marche, who was called Ucs lo Brus, was her knight, and she had loved and honored him as much as a lady can a knight. And one day he was courting her, and they made up a tenson *between them. And the Count of the Marche was saying that every true lover, if a lady gives him her love and takes him as her knight and friend, and if he's loyal and chivalrous with her, should have as much seigneury and authority over her as she over him; and my lady Maria held the view that the lover should have neither seigneury nor authority. En Gui d'Ussels was in the court of my lady Maria, and she, to draw him back into singing and happiness, composed a couplet in which she asked him whether it was right that the lover should have as much authority over the lady as the lady over him. And in this way my lady Maria provoked him into a* tenson, *and she said thus: "Gui d'Ussel, because of you I'm quite distraught . . ."*

Boutière, p. 212; H

Maria's life confirms the role described in the *razo*: she was an important patron of troubadours. Her mother was Helis de Castelnau, her father was Raimon II, Viscount of Turenne, one of the four viscounties of the Limousin. From the few spare facts we know about her she appears to have lived almost to the letter the life of a typical noblewoman of her time.

Like all women of her class, she was a pawn in the strategic interests of her father and her "clan." She and her two sisters were married off to the neighboring viscounties of Limoges, Comborn and Ventadorn (now Ventadour, in the Corrèze). This act of political precaution placed Maria de Turenne at a young age (somewhere between thirteen and twenty if the *Chronique de Geoffroy de Vigeois* is even vaguely to be trusted on her marriage date, which he gives as prior to 1183) at the center of one of the liveliest courts of Occitania. Ventadorn had long been a focus of troubadour culture, the great-grandfather of Maria's husband Ebles V having been the famous troubadour Ebles II, a contemporary of Guilhem de Poitou. Ebles III, his son, had been the patron of Bertran de Born (see p. 30), who in 1182 has sung the praises of Maria and her sisters as "las tres de Torena."[17] Maria herself was patron to many troubadours, among whom were Pons de Capdoill, the Monk of Montaudon, Savaric de Mauleon, Guiraut de Calanson, Gaucelm Faidit and Gui d'Ussel,[18] with whom she exchanged the *tenson* on p. 99 which is the only extant sample of her writing. The poem in all likelihood was written prior to 1209, the year in which the papal legate, according to Gui's *vida*, forbade him to continue writing.

Very little is known about Maria's life at Ventadorn. The *razo* paints the picture of a perfect literary hostess, almost a precursor of the *dame de salon*. It is easy to imagine periods of great activity in Maria's eagle-nest *château* – banquets, song fests, costuming and dances – but it should also be remembered that the isolated castle must have passed many a bleak month unvisited, with only such entertainment as the members of the court could themselves provide. Perhaps it was in "dry spells" such as these that a patron would find herself become a poet.

Maria is last attested in an act of 1221 in which, along with her two sons and two of her brothers, she witnessed her husband's vows as a monk entering the Cistercian abbey of Grandmont.[19] Already in her forties, if not her fifties, Maria was still under the guardianship of men; she had no legal status of her own.

Maria may well have lived on, presiding over her court at Ventadorn for many years, but we have no trace of her after her husband became a monk.

Alamanda
Source of Poem: Schultz-Gora, p. 19; AR

There is no *vida* of Alamanda, and the only piece of information
we have about her comes through the life of Guiraut de Bornelh,
with whom she composed this *tenson*. His dates are c. 1130–
post 1200[20], so that we can safely place her in the second half
of the twelfth century. Beyond that, there is only one additional
clue. In a *razo* to the *tenson* between Alamanda and Guiraut she
is called "una domna de Gascoina . . . N'Alamanda d'Estancs."
Again, if the *vidas* are to be trusted on geography, we can go
the slight step further of calling her a Gascon, and take Boutière's
suggestion that she was from the town of Estang, *cant.* of
Cataubon, *arrond.* of Condom (Gers).[21] This bit of information
is useful only in demonstrating the extent of troubadour poetry
and the presence of women troubadours in a large area of
southern France.

Scholars have debated back and forth on the authorship of
this poem, and their arguments fall into three camps: those who
say she alone wrote it, those who say he alone wrote it, and those
who consider it a genuine specimen of a *tenson*. Time is unlikely
to yield up an answer.

Garsenda
Source of Poem: Schultz-Gora, p. 21; FT

All traces of Garsenda would have been lost were it not for the
vidas of the troubadours Gui de Cavaillon and Elias de Barjols,
both of whom, according to their *vidas*, loved her. The *vida* of
the latter, after naming the poet's patron as "the count Alphonse
of Provence," refers to her as "the Countess my lady Garsenda,
wife of the Count"; that of Gui de Cavaillon calls her "Countess
Garsenda, wife of him who was the brother of the King of
Aragon." These two references permit us to establish that a
certain Garsenda was the wife of Alphonse II of Provence, whose

brother was Pedro II of Aragon. But how do we know that this Garsenda was a poet, and that she was the author of the poem attributed to her. We don't know for sure, but there is good reason to believe she was.

Her poem is given in two manuscripts. In one it appears anonymously, in the other it is attributed to "la contessa de Proessa." Garsenda was not the only Countess of Provence. Another possible identity for the poet would be Douce, the only daughter and sole heir of Raimon-Berengar II; however, Douce, who died in 1172, seems to have held the title only technically, since it was usurped from her while she was still a girl, and she lived out her life in virtual seclusion, far from the centers of troubadour culture.[22] Garsenda's immediate predecessor in the title was Richilde, wife of Raimon V of Toulouse; but Richilde lost her title when Raimon V was defeated by Alphonse II of Aragon, whose claims to Provence were more legitimate. Out of this confusion the only genuine alternative identity for the Countess of Provence would be Garsenda's daughter-in-law, Beatritz de Savoy, who became Countess when she married Raimon-Berengar the IV (or V, depending on the source), Garsenda's son, in 1220. In choosing between Beatritz and Garsenda, the close connections of Garsenda and her husband with many troubadours, and the fact that Elias de Barjols dedicated at least four poems to her (nos. V, VI, VII, and VIII of S. Stonski's edition of his poems), persuade me that Garsenda is the likelier candidate of the two.

All accounts agree that it was her grandfather, Count Guilhem de Forcalquier, who gave her in marriage to Alphonse II of Provence in 1193.[23] By this date her father must already have been dead; otherwise her grandfather would not have negotiated her marriage. There is a will of a Bernard de Forcalquier dated 1168.[24] A Guigo de Forcalquier is attested in 1149, but he is too early to have been the father of a woman first married in 1193. Thus, Garsenda was probably the daughter of Bernard, and could not have been born after 1168. Her mother's name is unanimously given as Garsenda de Forcalquier; there is no ground for supposing *her* to be the author of the poem, since she never held the title Countess of Provence.

As the wife of Alphonse II and in her own right as a Forcalquier, Garsenda belonged to two of the most powerful and important noble families of southern France. It is for this reason that we have relatively abundant information on her life.

It is not difficult to understand the reasoning behind the marriage of a daughter of the Forcalquiers to the heir of the house of Provence. In 1189, after an extremely bloody war provoked by the refusal of a nobleman named Boniface de Castellane to render homage to the Count, a number of other powerful *senhors* were humbled alongside him into recognizing Alphonse as their sovereign, "all becoming vassals of him whom they had formerly considered as their equal."[25] In the light of these events, Garsenda's marriage four years later is transparent: she was the token of her family's subjection.

Her grandfather, however, was shrewd; he must deeply have despised the husband he was forced by circumstance to choose for his granddaughter. To begin with, he reserved for himself the right of *usufructus* on the enormous county that was Garsenda's dowry. Then, shortly after her marriage, angry with Alphonse for an unknown reason, he revoked part of the rights to Forcalquier and gave them to Garsenda's sister, who in turn took them in marriage to the Dauphin of the Viennois. This manipulation began a war between Garsenda's grandfather and husband, in which the count of Toulouse sided with the old Guillem and the house of Aragon with Alphonse.[26]

Yet in the midst of all this intrigue and what at times must have been terror, the court of Alphonse II was a thriving cultural center where Garsenda played the role of patron to a number of poets. However, it is suggested in Boutière's comments on the *vida* of Elias de Barjols that this activity was probably begun after the death of Alphonse II, in 1209.

In 1209, in any event, began Garsenda's active political life, which was to last at least ten years. Accounts do not agree on whether she was able to control the upbringing of her infant son, over whom everyone was fighting. It seems that her Aragonese in-laws, fearing her natural enough loyalties to Forcalquier, usurped her rights as guardian of her son, whom they took to Spain and whose custody she did not regain until 1213, when her brother-in-law King Pedro was killed in the Battle of Muret. Beginning in 1209 Garsenda was regent of Provence, living in Aix and ruling until 1217 or 1220.

The marriage of her son brought Garsenda's active life to an end. She was probably in her early fifties when in 1222 or 1225 she retired to the abbey of La Celle (*cant.* de Brignolles, Var). Balaguer's report that she was still alive in 1257 is not impossible, even though she would then have been in her eighties.[27] If Balaguer is correct, it was in an act of 1257 that Garsenda made a donation to the church of St. Jean (in Aix?) on the condition that three priests be kept to pray for her soul and that of her dead husband.

In 1230, Raimon-Berengar the IV, Garsenda's son, founded the town of Barcelonnette in the Alps, "in memory of his forebears, the counts of Barcelona."[28] But Barcelonnette (Alpes-de-Hte. Provence) is also only fifty miles from Forcalquier, the young count's maternal legacy.

Isabella
Source of Poem: Schultz-Gora, p. 22; O

As in the case of so many of the women troubadours, every clue we have on Isabella comes through the life of Elias Cairel, the troubadour with whom she exchanged her *tenson*.

Cairel was from a small town near Périgord, and worked gold and silver and designed armor. The *vida* says that he sang badly, wrote badly, played the vielle badly and spoke even worse; but that he was good at copying music and words. He traveled to Romania and was in Salonika by 1207, going from there to Italy, where he spent the years 1215–1225.[29] It is there that he may have met Isabella if, as some scholars say, she was the daughter

of Boniface of Montferrat or of Marchesopulo Pelavicini. Boutière mentions Boniface (born c. 1160) as an important patron
of troubadours.[30] On the other hand, those who like the idea of
a romantic meeting in Romania have seen in her the daughter of
one Guido Marchesopulo, lord of Bodonitza in Thessaly, who
went to Romania in 1210.[31] But all this is pure conjecture, aside
from the fact that all three men had daughters named Isabella.

A possible clue to her identity may lie in the identity of the
patriarch Ivan (line 40 of the poem), certainly a reference to a
patriarch of the Eastern Church.

Lombarda

Source of Poem: Jules Véran, Les Poétesses provençales du moyen-âge
jusqu'à nos jours, *p. 90; H*

> *VIDA:*
> *Lady Lombarda was from Toulouse, a lady noble and beautiful, and
> gracious in her person and accomplished. And she knew how to write
> poems, and she composed beautiful verses about love. Don Bernartz
> N'Arnautz, brother of the count of Armanhac, heard tell of her
> goodness and her worth, and he came to Toulouse to see her. And he
> stayed with her in great intimacy and courted her and was her good
> friend. And he made these verses about her and sent them to her, to
> her house, and then he got on his horse without seeing her and went
> back to his own land . . . .*
>
> Boutière, p. 416; H

This *vida* fast turns into a *razo*, the *jongleur*'s paraphrase of the
song he was about to sing. But from it we get two important facts:
that Lombarda was from Toulouse, and that the Bernart Arnaut
with whom she exchanged her clever lines was the brother of
the Count of Armagnac, which allows him, and by extension
Lombarda, to be dated.

Bernart Arnaut did not succeed his brother as count of Armagnac until 1217; thus, according to Alfred Jeanroy, the poem
has to have been composed before that date since the *razo* calls
him "brother of the count."

If, at the very latest, the poem was composed in 1216, Lombarda must have been at least twenty by that point: she is credited with a literary reputation and described as a "noble lady" (i.e., married). Her writing shows her ability to handle the intricacies of *trobar clus* (see p. 75). I am therefore inclined to say that she could hardly have been born much later than 1190, and that she was in all likelihood born earlier.

As to her name, there is less reason to think her Italian, as some scholars have, than to consider her the daughter of a banking family. In the Middle Ages the name Lombard was a sign of those who dealt in money.

Castelloza

Source of Poems: I: Schultz-Gora, p. 23; A. II: Schultz-Gora, p. 23; A. III: Schultz-Gora, p. 24; A.

VIDA:

> Na Castelloza was from Auvergne, a noble lady, wife of Turc de Mairona. And she loved N'Arman de Breon and made up songs about him. And she was a lady very gay and very accomplished and very beautiful. And here are written down some of her songs.
>
> Boutière, p. 333; AIK

It is disappointing that Castelloza must remain almost a total mystery when she is one of the finest of the women troubadours. The earliest figure with the name Turc de Mairona is mentioned around 1225. Boutière reports that Mairona is the castle of Meyronne (*com.* de Venteuges, *cant.* de Saugues, *arrond.* du Puy, Hte. Loire), and that one of its lords, having returned from a successful Crusade to the East some time after 1220, gave himself that epithet.[32] All this would tell us only that Castelloza, if indeed she was the wife of this man, must have lived in the first half of the thirteenth century, somewhere in the area around Le Puy.

For the record, there is a Castellotz in Aragon where the troubadour Bertran de Born found patronage.[33] This fact, however, would contradict the *vida* statement that Castelloza was from the Auvergne.

Clara d'Anduza

Source of Poem: Schultz-Gora, p. 26; C. A. F. Mann, Die Werke der Troubadours in provenzalischer Sprache, *Berlin 1846, vol. III, p. 210.*

Clara does not have a *vida* but she is mentioned in the *razo* to a poem by Uc de Saint Circ, the thirteenth-century biographer (still alive in 1253) who has been credited with the authorship of most of the *vidas.*

In brief, the *razo* tells how Uc was the lover of Clara d'Anduza, and how he made her famous by writing songs in her honor, so that "there was not a single lady in that region – *en totas aquellas encontradas* – who did not have intimate and friendly relations with her, or who didn't send her letters, greetings and presents out of admiration and respect." But a vile friend of Clara's, Na Ponsa, grew jealous of this situation, and put into Uc's head the notion that Clara had another lover. He immediately broke with Clara, and became the lover of Ponsa. This, however, did not last long, for Uc found out through still another friend of Clara's that Clara had in fact always been faithful to him. A desperate man, he tried to win her back by writing this poem which goes . . . And so the *razos* go.

All we know for certain about Uc de Saint Circ is that he was from a village in the Lot, which would make him a near enough neighbor of Anduze (in the Gard) for the relationship recounted in the *razo* to be possible. Clara d'Anduza was probably related to Bernard d'Anduza (d. 1223), whose son, her son or brother, sided with Toulouse during the Albigensian Crusade.

Bieiris de Romans

Source of Poem: Schultz-Gora, p. 28; T

Bieiris de Romans is perhaps the most mysterious figure among the women troubadours. Scholars have resorted to the most ingenious arguments to avoid concluding that she is a woman writing a love poem to another woman.

Some have contended that the poem is a literary exercise, while others have seen it as a present from a woman to her friend, with the amorous tone simply a sign of flattery. Another interpretation makes Bieiris a *senhal* adopted by a man to show his esteem for women. (That is, by taking a woman's name one pays homage to the entire sex.) Still another interpretation is that the poem is religious, both women's names being spiritual symbols: Bieiris the forerunner of Dante's Beatrice, Maria the Virgin Mary. This last interpretation is rather difficult to support given the passionate vocabulary of the poem.

Schultz-Gora contended that the name Bieiris could be a corruption of Alberico de Romano, who was an Italian troubadour of the thirteenth century. In a conversation with the author, Charles Camproux refuted Schultz-Gora by demonstrating the linguistic process through which Beatrice might become Bieiris.

Romans is the canton capital of the *arrondissement* of Valence (Drôme), not far from Die and Orange. From this same town was Folquet de Romans, whose *vida* calls him a *joglar* (thus not a nobleman). Boutière places him in the first half of the thirteenth century.[34] But whether there is any relation between Folquet and Bieiris that would enable us to place her with greater accuracy remains to be seen.

Guillelma de Rosers
Source of Poem: Schultz-Gora, p. 27; IOM

Our information on Guillelma de Rosers comes through the *vida* of her troubadour-lover, Lanfrancs Cigala, and from an anonymous *chanson* in her honor, "Quan Proensa ac perduda proeza," which laments the long stay of Guillelma, "la flor de cortezia," in Genoa.[35]

Lanfrancs Cigala was a Genoese lawyer and well-known troubadour. Evidently the anonymous poem was by someone else, perhaps someone back in Provence. Cigala first appears in documents of the year 1241, when he was envoy to Raimon-Berengar

of Provence, but some of his poems can be dated before that.[36]
Schultz-Gora believes that the *tenson* between Guillelma and
Lanfrancs was exchanged in Genoa, but this is not necessarily so
since it could just as easily have been composed while Lanfrancs
Cigala was in Provence.

There are several possibilities for the location of Rosers. There
is a Rosières near Largentière in the Ardèche, about twelve miles
from Montélimar, and a Roziers near Millau, in the *département*
of Lozère. There is also a Rougiers (*cant.* de St. Maximin, *arrond.*
de Brignolles, Var), a good candidate on two counts: first, its
etymological closeness to Rosers (which contains the root *ros*,
red = French *rouge*); and second, its proximity to Italy and therefore to Monaco, where Lanfrancs Cigala is said to have been
assassinated in 1278.[37] It is also the only one of the three towns
located in Provence proper, to return to the first line of the
anonymous poem quoted above.

Domna H.
Source of Poem: Schultz-Gora, p. 25; IO

Nothing at all is known about her. People have made all sorts of
suggestions of names beginning with H, but it seems a pointless
search – there are, after all, so many.

Rosin is certainly a *senhal*, a short form of *rosinhol*, nightingale.
This was a commonly used *senhal*, and sheds no light on the
identity of either Domna H. or her male partner.

Alais, Iselda and Carenza
Source of Poem: Schultz-Gora, p. 28; Q

Nothing at all is known about any of these three women. Their
poem suggests that they are noble, but their identities remain
obscure. The word *serors*, sister, in line two might be taken to

mean "nun." Perhaps the two sisters are two young women in a convent, writing for advice to a more experienced woman on the outside.

The poem is extremely allegorical in places, and extremely practical and frank in others. It is unique in the literature of the period, and would benefit from further study and interpretation.

The Anonymous Poems
Anonymous I *(Source: Schultz-Gora, p. 28; C)*

This *tenson* has been attributed in many editions to the Countess of Dia. However, the grounds for making her its author are slim. Some scholars have pointed out the similarity between the opening line, "Amics, en gran cossirier," with that of her *chanson* "Estat ai en greu cossirier." The text is given in three manuscripts, two of which place it directly under the name of Raimbaut d'Orange, and one which prints it in the list of his poems. I have included it in this collection because, whether or not the female voice is that of the Countess of Dia, it is a well-written part; and because of this, it may indeed have been written by her.

Anonymous II *(Source: Schultz-Gora, p. 29; R)*

Schultz-Gora was the first to edit this poem, and he published it among his Anonyma. He suggests a connection between it and the poem of Alamanda (see p. 103) because of the similarity of themes – a woman intervenes on behalf of a man who is languishing from love-sickness. Since we have the same general idea in the poem between Almucs and Iseut (p. 93), I am inclined to see it as a whole genre, rather than to make a definite connection between the poems.

The lack of personal reference in the poem makes it impossible to date it or attempt attribution.

Anonymous III *(Source: Schultz-Gora, p. 30; I)*

Apparently this poem was never edited before Schultz-Gora.

FOOTNOTES

Introduction

1. Claude Marks, *Pilgrims, Heretics and Lovers* (New York: Macmillan, 1975), p. x.
2. Charles Camproux, *Le Joy d'amor des troubadours* (Montpellier: Causse & Castelnau, 1965), p. 101.
3. C. S. Lewis, *The Allegory of Love* (1936; rept. Oxford: Oxford University Press, 1970), p. 12.
4. See L. T. Topsfield, *Troubadours and Love* (Cambridge, England: Cambridge University Press, 1975), and James Wilhelm, *Seven Troubadours* (University Park, Pennsylvania: Pennsylvania State University Press, 1970).
5. Sybille Harksen, *La Femme au moyen-âge* (Leipzig: Edition Leipzig, 1974), p. 13.
6. Simone de Beauvoir, "Simone de Beauvoir interroge Jean-Paul Sartre," in *Arc* vol. 61 (Aix-en-Provence, 1975), p. 3.

Historical Background

1. Pressure for female dowering stemmed from the need to increase land holdings diminished by generations of being parceled out to numerous sons. While primogeniture was meant to guarantee the patrilineal descent of property within a single family, in practice lesser grants were often made to second, third and fourth-born sons, etc., so that the largest fiefs were gradually reduced to ever smaller "patrimonies." By means of his wife's dowry a man could, with luck, vastly increase his holdings.
2. On survivals of matrilineal descent in Occitania, see Charles Camproux, *Le Joy d'amor des troubadours* (Montpellier: Causse & Castelnau, 1965), p. 96. For related references, see Marc Bloch, *Feudal Society*, trans. L. A. Manyon (1940; rept. Chicago: University of Chicago Press, 1961), I, 137.
3. Saint-Allais, ed., *L'Art de vérifier les dates* (Paris: 1818), II, p. 107.
4. Camproux, *Le Joy d'amor*, p. 96.
5. Gaston Richard, *La Femme dans l'histoire* (Paris: 1909), p. 278.
6. Camproux, *Le Joy d'amor*, pp. 69–92.
7. Sybille Harksen, *La Femme au moyen-âge* (Leipzig: Edition Leipzig, 1974), p. 9.
8. Friedrich Engels, *The Origin of the Family, Private Property and the State* (1884; New York: International Publishers, 1973), p. 35;

Harksen, *La Femme au moyen-âge*, p. 13. A variation of the *ius primae noctis*, less brutal but equally humiliating, allowed the lord to ceremoniously stride over the bride and the marriage bed as a sign of his authority.

9. René Nelli, *La Vie quotidienne des cathares du Languedoc au XIIIe siècle* (Paris: Hachette, 1969), p. 82.

10. Maurice Keen, *The Pelican History of Medieval England* (Penguin Books, 1969), p. 84.

11. Claude Marks, *Pilgrims, Heretics and Lovers* (New York: Macmillan, 1975), p. 111.

12. Henri Pirenne, *Economic and Social History of Medieval Europe* trans. I. E. Klegg (New York: Harcourt, 1956), p. 51.

13. Luce Pietri, *Epoques médiévales (V^e–XVe siècles)* (Paris: Bordas/Laffont, 1971), p. 525.

14. Massas e brans, elms de color,
    escutz trauchar e desguarnir
    veirem a l'entrar de l'estor
    e maintz vassals ensems ferir,
    don anaran arratge
    chaval dels mortz e dels nafratz.
    E quan er en l'estorn entratz,
    chascus om de paratge
    no pens mas d'asclar chaps e bratz,
    que mais val mortz que vius sobratz.

15. Pietri, *Epoques médiévales,* p. 52.

16. Dels huelhs ploret josta la fon
    e del cor sospiret preon.
    "Ihesus," dis elha, "reys del mon,
    per vos mi creys ma grans dolors,
    quar vostra anta mi cofon,
    quar li mellor de tot est mon
    vos van servir, mas a vos platz.

    . . . ben o crey
    que Deus aya de mi mercey
    en l'autre segle per jassey,
    quon assatz d'autres peccadors;
    mas say mi tolh aquelha rey
    don joys mi crec; mas pauc mi tey
    que trop s'es de mi alonhatz."

17. Friedrich Heer, *The Medieval World*, trans. Janet Sondheimer (1961; New York: Mentor Books, 1962), p. 136.

18. Marks, *Pilgrims, Heretics and Lovers,* p. 489.

19. David Herlihy, "Women in Medieval Society," Smith History Lecture for 1971 (Houston, Texas: University of St. Thomas, 1971), pp. 10–11.
20. The most recent work on the role of women in the medieval church is Joan Morris, *The Lady Was A Bishop* (New York: Macmillan, 1973).
21. Putnam, *The Lady*, p. 130.
22. There were women poets writing in Arabic in Andalusia in the eleventh century. Practically no work has been done on them, and there is no indication yet as to whether they compare in number with the women troubadours. The only source on them is Al-Maqquari, *History of the Mohammedan Dynasties of Spain*, (London, 1840), Vol. I, pp. 161–167, which gives the names Kasmúnah (a Jew), Ummu-l-sa'd; Al-ghosániyyah, Al-'arúdhiyyah, and Hafsah 'Ar-rakúniyyah, among others.

Courtly Love: a new interpretation

1. Charles Homer Haskins, *The Renaissance of the Twelfth Century* (1927; rept. New York: Meridian Books, 1968).
2. For a thorough exposition of the history of medieval poetry prior to the troubadours, see Peter Dronke, *Medieval Latin and the Rise of European Love-Lyric* (Oxford: Clarendon Press, 1968), Vol. I: Problems and Interpretations.
3. Anc mais no poc hom faissonar
con's, en voler ni en dezir
ni en pensar ni en cossir;
aitals joy no pot par trobar,
e qui be.l volria lauzar
d'un an no y poiri' avenir.
4. Totz joys li deu humiliar,
et tota ricor obezir
mi dons, per son belh aculhir
e per son belh plazent esguar;
e deu hom mais cent ans durar
qui.l joy de s'amor pot sazir.
5. A Dieu coman Bel Estar
e plus la ciutat d'Aurenza
e Glorïet' e.l Caslar
e lo seignor de Proenza
e tot can vol mon ben lai;
e l'arc on son fag l'assai . . . .
6. Dronke, *Medieval Latin* is the clearest and best-documented statement of this view.

7. C. S. Lewis, *The Allegory of Love* (1936; rept. Oxford: Oxford University Press, 1970), p. 12.

8. René Nelli, *L'Erotique des troubadours* (1963; rept. Paris: Collection 10/18, 1974), II, 257.

9. The classic statement on the links between Arab and Hispano-Arab poetry and the courtly love lyric of Occitania is Alois Richard Nykl, *Hispano-Arab Poetry and Its Relations With the Old Provençal Troubadours* (Baltimore: 1946). However, research needs to be done on why Arab poets idealized the lady.

10. Nelli, *Erotique*, II, p. 264.

11. Nelli, *loc. cit.*

12. Charles Camproux, *Le Joy d'amor des troubadours* (Montpellier: Causse & Castelnau, 1965), p. 78.

13. Nelli, *Histoire du Languedoc* (Paris: Hachette, 1974), p. 56.

14. Robert Briffault, *The Troubadours* (1948; Bloomington, Indiana: Indiana University Press, 1965), p. 53.

15. Briffault, p. 78.

16. Maurice Valency, *In Praise of Love* (1958; rept. New York: Macmillan, 1961), p. 110.

17. Emily James Putnam's classic work, *The Lady* (1910; rept. Chicago, University of Chicago Press, 1969), devotes a whole chapter to "The Lady of the Castle." See also, Sybille Harksen, *La Femme au moyen-âge* (Leipzig, 1974).

18. Denys Hay, *The Medieval Centuries* (1953; rept. New York: Harper Torchbooks, 1965), p. 41.

19. Tan am midons e la tenh car,
   e tan la dopt' e la reblan
   c'anc de me no.lh quer ni re no.lh man.
   Pero ilh sap mo mal e ma dolor,
   e can li plai, mi fai ben et onor,
   e can li plai, eu m'en sofert ab mens,
   per so c'a leis no.n avenha blastens.

20. Technically *midons* is not a *senhal*, but its oblique usage – it was never used as a direct form of address – and syntactic oddness caused it to function as one. The term may have grown out of incorrect grammar, but the connection with the Arab forms needs to be more fully studied. The most recent survey of possible derivations of *midons* is Mary Hackett, "Le Problème de *midons*, "*Mélanges de philologie romane dédiés à la mémoire de Jean Boutière*, ed. I. Cluzel and F. Pirot (Liège: Editions Solédi, 1971, pp. 285–294.)

21. No posc dir mal de leis, que non i es;
   qu'e.l n'agra dih de joi, s'eu li saubes;
   mas no li sai, per so m'en lais de dire.

22. E s'ieu sai ren dir ni faire,
    ilh n'aia.l grat, que sciensa
    m'a donat e conoissensa,
    per qu'ieu sui gais e chantaire.
23. Bona domna, re no.us deman
    mas que.m prendatz per servidor,
    qu'e.us servirai com bo senhor,
    cossi que del gazardo m'an.
24. En totas res sembli ben cavallier;
    si.m sui, e sai d'amor tot son mestier
    e tot aisso qu'a drudairi' abau;
    anc en cambra non ac tan plazentier
    ni ab armas tan mal ni tan sobrier,
    don m'am' e.m tem tals que no.m ve ni m'au.
25. E s'aissi pert s'amistat,
    be.m tenh per dezeretat
    d'amor, e ja Deus no.m do
    mais faire vers ni chanso.
26. De l'aiga que dels olhs plor,
    escriu salutz mais de cen,
    que tramet a la gensor
    et a la plus avinen.
    Manhtas vetz m'es pois membrat
    de so que.m fetz al comjat:
    que.lh vi cobrir sa faisso,
    c'anc no.m poc dir oc ni no.
27. Alfred Jeanroy, *La Poésie lyrique des troubadours* (Toulouse and Paris: Didier-Privat, 1934), and *Les Origines de la poésie lyrique en France au moyen-âge* (1889; Paris: Champion, 1965).
28. Robert Briffault, *The Troubadours* (1948; Bloomington, Indiana, 1965).
29. Denis de Rougemont, *Love in the Western World* (1939; New York: Harper and Row, 1974).
30. Jacques Madaule, *Le Drame albigeoise et l'unité française* (1961; rept. Paris: Editions Gallimard, 1973), p. 25.
31. Briffault, *The Troubadours,* pp. 96–125.
32. Bernart de Ventadorn, according to his *vida,* was banished from the court of Ebles III, Viscount of Ventadorn, after his love for the viscountess was discovered; the *vida* of Peire Vidal reports that his tongue was slashed because he was found to be the lover of the wife of a lord of St. Gilles. Even if these stories are untrue or hyperbolic, they reveal the moral attitudes of the society on which the troubadours depended for their living.

33. Harksen, *La Femme au moyen-âge.*
34. Ground-breaking work in anthropology is beginning to reveal startling cross-cultural parallels: "Unlike the two or three generations of a woman's domestic group, the male peer group often has no natural criteria that uniquely determine membership, order relationships, or establish chains of command. Instead, order within male groups and in the social world in general, is felt to be a cultural product, and men elaborate systems of norms, ideals, and standards of evaluation that permit them to order relationships among themselves. If 'becoming a man' is, developmentally, an 'achievement,' social groups elaborate the criteria for that achievement and create the hierarchies we associate with an articulated social order. Insofar as achievement in this sense is a perquisite of manhood, then men create and control a social order in which they compete as individuals. Womanhood, by contrast, is more of a given for the female, and in most societies we find relatively few ways of expressing the differences among women . . .", Michelle Zimbalist Rosaldo in *Women, Culture and Society* (ed. Michelle Zimbalist Rosaldo and Louise Lamphere, Stanford University Press, 1974).
35. Si la bela cui sui profers
    me vol onrar
    d'aitan que.m denhe sofertar
    qu'eu sia sos fis entendens,
    sobre totz sui rics e manens.
36. I am indebted for my first thinking along these lines to E. Köhler's "Observations historiques et sociologiques sur la poésie des troubadours," *Cahiers de civilisation médiévale* VII (1964), in particular to the following statement: ". . . 'far-off love' (*l'amor de lonh*) is no less, in the final analysis, than the sublimated projection of the material and social situation of the low nobility."
37. Tot iorn meillur et esmeri
    car la gensor serv e coli
    del mon, so.us dic en apert.
38. Since the Arab poets had employed a similar term in addressing the lady, it may be worthwhile to note that Arab custom prohibited the mention of a woman's name in public; this may be seen as a classic illustration of an avoidance taboo – i.e., the prohibition against mentioning anything too powerful or too contaminated, which is found in a number of diverse cultures. Perhaps on a subconscious level this sense of stigma was carried over into the poems of the troubadours. Cf. Simone de Beauvoir,". . . respect is the sublimation of an original disgust." (*The Second Sex,* p. 184).
39. Cf. A. J. Denomy, *The Heresy of Courtly Love* (New York: Macmillan, 1958).

40. Charles Camproux, "La Mentalité 'spirituelle' chez Peire Cardenal,"
    Cahiers de Fanjeaux No. 10, Centre d'études historiques de Fanjeaux
    (Toulouse: Editions Privat, 1975); R. Manselli, "Les Mendiants en
    pays d'oc au XIIIᵉ siècle," *Cahiers de Fanjeaux No. 8* (1973).

The Women Troubadours
1. The troubadour Bernart de Ventadorn, by tradition the son of
   servants of Ebles III, received his name from the lord of the castle.
   He was not related to Maria de Ventadorn.
2. Emily James Putnam, *The Lady* (1910; rept. Chicago: University of
   Chicago Press, 1969), p. 127.
3. Charles Camproux, *Le Joy d'amor des troubadours* (Montpellier:
   Causse & Castelnau, 1965).

Biographies
1. Walter Pattison, *The Life and Works of the Troubadour Raimbaut
   d'Orange* (Minneapolis: 1952).
2. Pattison, p. 12.
3. Pattison, p. 13.
4. Saint-Allier, ed., *L'Art de vérifier les dates* (Paris: 1818), IV, 255.
   Henceforth cited as *AVD*.
5. *AVD*, *loc. cit.*
6. *AVD*, *loc. cit.*
7. P. Anselme, *Histoire généalogique et chronologique des pairs de
   France* (Paris: 1728), II, 187.
8. Dom Brial, ed., *Recueil des historiens des Gaules et de la France*
   (Paris: 1806–1904), XIV, 427.
9. Anselme, II, 187.
10. Pattison, p. 15.
11. Anselme, II, 240.
12. Jean Mouzat, *Les Poèmes de Gaucelm Faidit* (Paris: A. G. Nizet,
    1965), p. 31.
13. Mouzat, p. 31.
14. Aimo Sakari, "Azalais de Porcairages, le 'joglar' de Raimbaut
    d'Orange," *Neuphilologische Mitteilungen* (Helsinki: 1949), vol. 50,
    pp. 23–24, 56–87, 174–98.
15. See note 1.
16. J. Boutière and A. H. Schutz, *Biographies des troubadours* (Paris:
    A. G. Nizet, 1964), p. 341.
17. S. Stronski, *La Légende amoureuse de Bertran de Born* (Paris: 1914),
    p. 38.
18. Mouzat, p. 16.
19. Stronski, p. 44.

20. Boutière, p. 42.
21. Boutière, p. 45.
22. *AVD*, II, 244.
23. Boutière, p. 216; *AVD*, II, 245; S. Stronski, "Notes sur quelques troubadours et protecteurs des troubadours," *Revue des langues romanes* (Montpellier: 1907), V^e série, vol. X.
24. Anselme, II, 241.
25. *AVD*, II, 244.
26. *AVD*, II, 24.
27. Victor Balaguer, *Historia política y literaria de los trovadores* (Madrid: 1878), p. 60.
28. Balaguer, p. 60.
29. Boutière, p. 253.
30. Boutière, p. 359.
31. Oscar Schultz-Gora, *Die Provenzalischen Dichterinnen* (Leipzig: 1888), p. 11.
32. Boutière, p. 334.
33. Boutière, p. 117.
34. Boutière, p. 504.
35. The full text can be found in Schultz-Gora, *op. cit.*, p. 31.
36. Schultz-Gora, p. 16.
37. Boutière, p. 510.

SELECTED READING LIST

THE LIST which follows is a guide to the books which I have found to be the very best in a field particularly rich in distinguished scholarship; more comprehensive bibliographies are given in several of the volumes cited. I have tried to keep the number of French books to a minimum. Those which do appear are excellent and still untranslated. Almost all the books included are currently available in paperback.

Books on women in the Middle Ages are few and far between. More need to be written.

Robert Briffault's *The Troubadours* (1948; English translation, Bloomington, Indiana: Indiana University Press, 1965) remains the outstanding introduction to the poetry and culture of the troubadours. Briffault, who knew Arabic, gives the best statement of the Arab theory, and provides solid chapters on the Albigensian Crusade and courtly love.

For Provençal, Frank R. Hamlin, Peter T. Ricketts and John Hathaway's *Introduction à l'étude de l'ancien provençal* (Geneva: Droz, 1967) is indispensable. The book begins with a concise grammar and moves quickly to simple texts from the *vidas* and poems of the major troubadours (including one poem by the Countess of Dia).

For further reading of troubadour poetry, the best anthology available in English is Frederick Goldin's *Lyrics of the Troubadours and Trouvères* (New York: Doubleday Anchor Books, 1963), which includes commentary and a thorough bibliography.

The companion volume, *German and Italian Lyrics of the Middle Ages*, is equally excellent. Ezra Pound's brilliant translations, particularly of Arnaut Daniel, are further from the letter but closer to the spirit of the Provençal. They can be found in Ezra Pound, *Translations* (New York: New Directions, 1953).

On the Middle Ages in general, several works are highly recommended. Friedrich Heer's *The Medieval World*, trans. Janet Sondheimer (New York: Mentor Books, 1962) is the most comprehensive and, though popularly written, is the best introduction to the period. Denys Hay's *The Medieval Centuries* (1953: New York, Harper Torchbooks, 1965) is a more specialized study with a focus on the development of institutions. Maurice Keen's *Pelican History of Medieval Europe* (Penguin Books, 1969) is more detailed than either Heer or Hay but not dry for a second.

On feudalism, Marc Bloch's *Feudal Society*, trans. L. A. Manyon (1940; rept. Chicago: University of Chicago Press, 1961) is the classic study; however François L. Ganshof's *Feudalism*, trans. Philip Grierson (1952; New York: Harper Torchbooks, 1964) is perhaps the better introductory volume on the subject.

The best survey of Occitanian history from pre-historic times to the present is René Nelli's *Histoire du Languedoc* (Paris: Hachette, 1974). On Occitanian literature, see Charles Camproux, *Histoire littéraire occitane* (Paris: Payot, 1971).

Of the many studies on Catharism and the Albigensian Crusade, the two most useful and most interesting are Jacques Madaule's *The Albigensian Crusade*, trans. Barbara Wall (London: Burns and Oates, 1967), and Zöe Oldenbourg's *Massacre at Monségur*, trans. Peter Green (London: Weidenfeld and Nicolson, 1961).

On courtly love, five books are particularly recommended. Charles Camproux', *Le Joy d'amor des troubadours* (Montpellier: Causse & Castelnau, 1965) is excellent on the philosophical and intellectual background, and devotes a whole chapter to the role of women in Occitanian society; Peter Dronke's *Medieval Latin and the Rise of European Love-Lyric* (Oxford: Clarendon Press, 1968) traces *fin' amors* as far back as ancient Egypt and as far from Occitania as Iceland to show that the troubadours' themes are universal; C. S. Lewis' *The Allegory of Love* (1936; rept. Oxford: Oxford University Press, 1970) is primarily a study of courtly love as it entered the English literary tradition; René Nelli's *L'Erotique des troubadours* (1963; rept. Paris: Collection 10/18, 1974) is an exhaustive and brilliant study on the sexual and psychological implications of courtly love; Maurice Valency's *In Praise of Love* (1958; rept. New York, Macmillan, 1961) weaves all these strands together.

The most recent and authoritative volume on the music of the troubadours is Hendrik van der Werf's *The Chansons of the Troubadours and Trouvères* (Utrecht: A. Oosthoek's Uitgeversmaatshappij, 1972), which includes transcriptions.

On women in the Middle Ages, see Emily James Putnam's superb *The Lady* (1910; rept. Chicago: University of Chicago Press, 1969) and Amy Kelly's biography of Eleanor of Aquitaine, *Eleanor of Aquitaine and the Four Kings* (Cambridge, Massachusetts: Harvard University Press, 1963).

As introductions to feminist thought and theory, three books are highly recommended. Simone de Beauvoir's *The Second Sex* (originally published in 1948; constantly reprinted and available in Bantam Books) is vast in scope and ground-breaking throughout; Sheila Rowbotham's *Women's Consciousness, Man's World* (Penguin Books, 1973), written from the vantage point of the present Women's Movement, is brilliant and concise; *Women, Culture and Society*, ed. Michelle Zimbalist Rosaldo and Louise Lamphere (Stanford: Stanford University Press, 1974) is a collection of papers by feminist anthropologists which shows the kind of revolutionary cultural analysis the Women's Movement has engendered.

Discography

One superb recording is recommended: *Chansons des Troubadours: Lieder und Spielmusik aus dem 12. Jahrhundert*, performed by the Studio der Frühen Musik on Telefunken in their series *Das Alte Werk* (SAWT 95673).

INDEX

Aigues-Mortes 23
Alamanda 64, 102–3, 170
alba, defined 40
Albigensian Crusade
— reasons for 57
— effect on women 58
— effect on troubadour poetry 58–61
Albigensian heresy. See Catharism.
Almucs de Castelnau 35, 64, 72, 92–3, 165–6
Andalusia 45–6
Arab poetry. See Hispano-Arab poetry.
Arabia 45–6
Arnaut Daniel 9, 43, 56
Auvergne 23, 26, 95, 119
Avignon 28, 93
Azalais de Porcairages 8, 16, 18, 40, 67, 68, 72, 94–5, 166–7

Beaucaire 28
Benedictines 26
Bernart de Ventadorn 15, 43, 51, 52, 53
Bertran de Born 30, 43, 99, 169
Béziers 23, 46, 58, 95
Bieiris de Romans 75, 132–3, 176–7
bourgeoisie 24, 29, 51

Capellanus, Andreas 15, 25
Carcassonne 23, 58
Castelloza 8, 66, 69, 72, 118–19, 175
Catharism 57–8
Cercamon 43, 52
chanson, defined 16
Charlemagne 21
Cistercians 26, 28
Clara d'Anduza 64, 72, 130–31, 176
Commerce
— growth of 28, 32
— relation to troubadour poetry 33
Conques, Ste. Foi de 26
Countess of Dia 8, 18, 67, 70, 82–3, 163–4, 179

Crusades
— reasons for 29–32
— effects on women 33–6
— influence on troubadour poetry 36–7

Dante 10, 15, 40, 61, 63
Dove's Neck Ring, The 46
Domna H. 72, 73, 178
dowries 22, 25

Eleanor of Aquitaine 24, 164
Elias Cairel 30, 64, 65, 111, 173
England 10, 28
Espiritals 59

feudalism
— basic tenets 20–21
— development 20–36
— as basis for troubadour poetry 21, 55–6
— position of women 22–6
fin' amors, defined 15, 38
Flanders 26, 28, 29

Garsenda 64, 75, 108–9, 170–73
Genoa 28
Gilbert de Nogent 32
Gregory VII, Pope 35
Gregorian Reform 35, 53
Gui d'Ussel 58, 73, 99, 168–9
Guilhem de Poitou 15, 35, 37–9, 43, 45, 46, 47
Guillelma de Rosers 64, 72, 73, 134–5, 177–8
Guiraut de Bornelh 43, 54, 64, 103

Hispano-Arab poetry
— influence on troubadour poetry 45–7
— image of woman in 45, 47, 50
— contacts between Spain and Occitania 45–7

Ile-de-France 29
Innocent III, Pope 57
Inquisition 25, 58
Isabella 64, 65, 67, 110–11, 173–4
Iseut de Capio 67, 92–3, 165–6
Italy 10, 28, 40, 58
ius primae noctis 25

Jaufré Rudel 43
Jerusalem 29, 32, 33
Jews 46
joglar, defined 16
jongleur, see *joglar*
joglaresa, female *joglar* 47
Justinian, code of 22

Lanfrancs Cigala 64, 73, 135
law
— status of women under
   Occitanian law 22–3
— Salic law 22
Limousin 23, 99
Lombarda 75, 114–15, 174–5
Lunel 46

Marcabru 33, 43
Maria de Ventadorn 58, 64, 72,
   73, 98–9, 168–9
Marie de France 36
Mariolatry
— rise of 58
— effect on troubadour poetry
   58–61
marriage
— status of women in 10, 24–5
— in early Middle Ages 22
Marseille 23
Merovingians 21
midons, defined 38
— discussion of function in
   troubadour poetry 50–1, 55–6
— syntactic description 50
Moissac, Abbaye de St. Pierre 26
Monségur 58
Montpellier 23, 26, 46, 166, 167

Narbonne 28, 46, 58
Nîmes 23, 28, 46

Orange 40, 97

pastorela, defined 40
Peire Cardenal 15, 58–9
Peire Vidal 15, 51, 52
Périgord 23
pilgrimages 28, 32
Pisa 28

Raimbaut d'Orange 43, 64, 81,
   95, 162, 164, 167, 179
Raimon IV of Toulouse 35
rape 25

razo, defined 99
Reconquista 45, 47

St. Gilles 28
St. Guilhem-le-Désert 26
St. John of Acre 33
St. Martin du Canigou 26
Salic law 22
Santiago de Compostela 28, 38–9
Scotland 28
Sénanque, Abbaye de 28
senhal, defined 50
slaves 21, 46
Spain 10, 28, 45–6, 58

tenson, defined 16
Theodisian Code 23
Theodora, wife of Emperor
   Justinian 22
Tibors 64, 65, 70, 80–1, 162
tornada, defined 16–17
Toulouse 23, 26, 28, 46, 49, 58
trobairitz, defined 12, 63
trobar clus, defined 75
Turks 32

Uc de St. Circ 176
Urban II, Pope 32, 35
usufructus 22

vassalage
— defined 21
— as central metaphor of
   troubadour poetry 21
Vauvert 46
Venice 28
vida, defined 8
Visigoths 22, 23

Waldensianism, See Catharism
women
— in early Middle Ages 10–12,
   22–5
— inheritance rights 22–4
— political power of 22–4
— Church attitude toward 12,
   35, 54, 57
— holding fiefs 23–4, 35
— peasant women 25
— rape 26
—Occitanian women 13–14,
   22–4, 35–6, 57